ÁINE CARLIN
THE NEW VEGAN

GREAT RECIPES, NO-NONSENSE ADVICE and SIMPLE TIPS

Photography by Nassima Rothacker

Kyle Books

For my Father, Hugo

First published in Great Britain in 2015 by
Kyle Books, an imprint of Kyle Cathie Ltd
192–198 Vauxhall Bridge Road
London SW1V 1DX
general.enquiries@kylebooks.com
www.kylebooks.com

10 9 8 7 6 5 4 3 2 1

ISBN 978 0 85783 308 2

Text © 2015 Áine Carlin
Design © 2015 Kyle Books
Photographs © 2015 Nassima Rothacker

Project Editor **Tara O'Sullivan**
Copy Editor **Abi Waters**
Editorial Assistant **Amberley Lowis**
Designer **Helen Bratby**
Photographer **Nassima Rothacker**
Illustrator **Stuart Simpson**
Food Stylist **Aya Nishimura**
Prop Stylist **Tony Hutchinson**
Production **Nic Jones** and **Gemma John**

A Cataloguing in Publication record for this title is
available from the British Library.

Colour reproduction by ALTA London
Printed and bound in China by C&C Offset Printing
Co., Ltd.

CONTENTS

WHY VEGAN?

It's a question I often ask myself – and the answer to which I occasionally need reminding of. Becoming vegan is both a simple and complex decision, and one so powerful it can dramatically change your life for the better. For many, leaving behind the familiarity of animal products can be daunting... after all, they have probably permeated your life for as long as you can remember. From infancy our parents have taught us which foods were 'good' and 'bad' and from there we developed our relationship with food, which can be called into question when you start considering veganism. So yes, you could say it's as simple and complex as that.

HEALTH

So why would anyone want to eschew a lifetime's dietary habits, and, more importantly, what is leading more and more of us to veganism – a lifestyle that, let's face it, often reeks of self righteousness and has a pretty 'crunchy' image problem to boot? Well, the only story I can really tell is my own, and that particular journey begins in the good old US of A. My husband and I were living in Chicago and, up until that point, we were enthusiastic carnivores with a pretty hefty dairy addiction on the side. When we moved to Chi-town for my husband's work, we thought we were in foodie heaven and lapped up every morsel that we came across, from Joe's Steakhouse to our favourite local diner on the corner of our road – nothing, and I mean nothing, was off limits. It was Reuben sandwiches and crab cakes galore, baby, and we didn't pause for one second to think about what it was doing to our bodies... or the animals we were gleefully consuming. To put it frankly, I simply didn't care.

Now, I should also say at this stage, that while we enjoyed dining out, I also loved (read LOVED!) to cook from scratch. Creating recipes and delicious dishes in my sanctuary (the kitchen) was my chill-out time. I could (and still do) spend hours thinking about food; what I might like to cook and when my next meal will be – call it an obsession, but food is definitely my 'thing'. Restricting myself to ingredients only of the plant variety would've seemed like madness to me five or six years ago and I honestly couldn't have conceived of going vegetarian, let alone vegan. Heck, I'm not even sure I knew what a 'vegan' was.

But when it all started to unravel and our health took a bit of a nose-dive, the first thing I looked to was our food habits – maybe because I instinctively knew the power food has on our physical and mental well being. Sure enough, staring me in the face was the answer to my lethargy, my brittle nails and hair, my extreme mood-swings, weight-gain and probably every other minor ailment I was experiencing.

Because for me, it wasn't about a life-changing disease (although for others it is), it was all those little niggles that began to mount up until they reached a point that couldn't (or at least shouldn't) be ignored. Think about it. Right now, are you in the best shape you could be? Do you feel in control of your body and understand what makes it tick? Does refined sugar hit you like a ton of bricks or does dairy leave you sluggish? If you think about it, you may find you're experiencing some of those annoying 'niggles' yourself.

I felt the only option was a concerted effort to clean up my lifestyle and that began with a serious inventory of what I actually was eating. If you're unsure yourself, go right now to your fridge and take a long hard look. If you're anything like I was, you'll probably find a considerable amount of dairy (or products containing some form of it), a hefty amount of meat and the odd bit of lack-lustre veg. Once you open your eyes and really start to read every label you'll be amazed how many animal by-products (such as gelatine and whey) have been secreted into your innocent-looking food. I know it sounds all very cloak and dagger (and it kinda is) but ultimately it is up to you to scour every product and take the decision as to whether you want whatever that hidden animal product might be in your system.

I like to think of it as taking back control of my vessel, and since doing so, I honestly haven't felt better. I err on the side of alkaline these days (animal products are incredibly 'acidic') although I still enjoy a moderate amount of sugar, caffeine, alcohol and white flour. I'm of the 'everything in moderation' school of thought (which probably sounds weird coming from a vegan) but I'm also acutely aware of the negative effects these things can have on the body. Much in the same way animal products behave, sugar, alcohol and refined white flour are all pretty sore on the system so I try to balance them out with green smoothies and nutrient-dense ingredients like quinoa and kale.

COMPASSION

Animal welfare is a huge (make that massive) part of my veganism. It pretty much surpasses my desire to stay healthy and is on an absolute par with helping to protect the environment – well, you can't really have one without the other, can you? Although it was initially the footnote to my plant-based diet, the more I learned about the food industry, the more I began to connect with what (and who) I was eating. If ever there was a lightbulb moment in my life, the realisation that I didn't need (or want) to eat animals was it.

This realisation is still the foundation of my veganism but one, I must admit, I find increasingly hard to talk about. Never wanting to be deemed 'preachy', I often shy away from saying what I really think on the matter because it's usually not something the general public want to hear. I've also realised on this journey of mine, that we're all built a little differently – and truthfully my demeanour doesn't lend itself well to controversy or dogmatism. It's just not me. So, if you're looking for slaughterhouse horror stories to sway you, you won't find them here. Sorry!

With that said, let me direct you to a wondrous invention called 'the internet'. It has all the information you could possibly need on factory farm practices, what happens to those discarded male chicks and how dairy cows are really treated. It's all there for you at the mere click of a button.

Whilst some people are all about highlighting the hidden truth of veganism, I'm about offering an alternative by way of living a more compassionate life. Of course, it would be foolish of me to make sweeping statements claiming that vegans don't like the taste or texture of meat, or don't relish the creamy unctuousness of a good brie (otherwise, why would there be so many substitutes?), but ultimately it's fair to say we would rather go without than see another animal suffer to feed our desires. And with so many vegan options now on the market, there is barely any sacrifice involved. It's why I do what I do. It's what drives me to create delicious food with that crucial 'umami' layer of flavour. I truly believe we *can* have our cake and eat it – and all without hurting any animals in the process.

Tradition, history and habit do not intrinsically make something 'right'. Sure, as cavemen we had to hunt animals in order to survive but guess what? We have evolved since the stone-age and no longer need to rely on our spears to catch dinner – much in the same way we choose to not rock about in loin cloths. Well, for the most part, ahem!

Although I am absolutely not at liberty to tell you what to eat or how to live your life, I hope you'll let me suggest another way that might just dissuade you from the meat aisle and get you excited about plants instead. You can't blame a girl for trying, eh?

ENVIRONMENT

My passion for the environment stems back to childhood. Whether it was Friends of the Earth or Greenpeace, I always had some cause to fight and proudly bore their stickers on my bedroom window for all to see. I remember eagerly taking part in sponsored walks and really believed I was making the world a slightly better place... who knows, maybe in my own small way I was. My environmentalist career may never have materialised, but as I continue to join the dots between the food we choose to eat and how it affects the world we live in, I'm more sure than ever that veganism is the path for me.

It's an overwhelming feeling to think that something as simple as stopping off at a fast food joint can have a ripple effect that reaches halfway around the planet, but, rest assured, it does. There are huge swathes of rainforest being flattened right now in order to house the livestock that will eventually lie in a burger bun. It's a burden that I no longer wanted on my shoulders, which is why I simply removed myself from the animal product equation.

From global warming and impending water shortages to the worrying decline of bees, our food demands are slowly but surely destroying the planet. I can't think of a better way to remedy the situation than to start with breakfast, lunch and dinner, can you? I bet if we collectively opted out of animal products for even a few days a week, we could turn this thing around in no time. Sounds pretty ambitious, I know, but I'm ever the optimist and I hope by the end of this book you will be, too.

WHAT
WELLNESS
MEANS
TO ME

'Wellness' is a term that gets thrown around a lot these days, but it is something that should be considered. Wellness, to me, is all encompassing. It's not just what we eat, but how we choose to live, the way we treat ourselves (and others), and how we approach each and every day. Whether it's laying a pretty table, lighting a scented candle, taking time to enjoy a cup of tea or simply watching an episode of my favourite programme during even the most hectic of days, I always endeavour to take pleasure in the small things... and often, that involves food. Veganism, for me, was simply an extension of this philosophy. Small decisions that, collectively speaking, have a large impact – not only for you, but for the world around you too. Instigating a positive change to my lifestyle was my way of making a regular proactive statement that sent out a subliminal message of respect and love. Put those vibes out often enough and you're bound to get something back in return. Can you say 'kumbayah'?

So yes, food is at the heart of my happiness (and indeed 'wellness'), but not just because it's fuelling my body. I've come to realise that, as soon as I began to respect this vessel I'm in and nourish it with all the right things, I was also inadvertently doing my part in helping the earth to heal and sheltering some of its inhabitants from unnecessary harm.

The nutrition side of things obviously plays a pivotal role in sustaining my love for this lifestyle and helps me thrive on a daily basis. Some people learning about veganism for the first time are concerned about missing out on vital nutrients, but they can all be found in vegan-friendly foods. I now don't have to think about my nutrient intake because it's become second nature and, truthfully, it's not as daunting (or tiresome) as it sounds. With that said, it's always helpful to have a starting point, so overleaf is a list of the best vegan sources of protein, calcium, iron etc. to get you started.

VEGAN SOURCES OF NUTRIENTS

PROTEIN
» Beans, including chickpeas (hummus), cannellini beans, black beans, red kidney beans, etc.
» Lentils
» Quinoa
» Buckwheat
» Chia seeds
» Soy products, including tofu, soya milk, soya yogurt, etc.
» Hemp products, including hemp milk and hemp seeds
» Nuts and related products, including walnuts, pecans, pumpkin seeds, almonds, cashews, nut butters and tahini
» Green peas
» Oats
» Tempeh

CALCIUM
» Kale and other leafy greens
» Blackstrap molasses
» Sesame seeds and tahini
» Almond butter
» Broccoli
» Sweet potato
» Blackberries
» Oranges
» Dried apricots
» Dates
» Figs
» Aduki beans
» Soy products, including soya milk and tofu

IRON
» Blackstrap molasses
» Leafy greens
» Dried fruit
» Dark chocolate
» Tomato purée
» Wholegrains, including quinoa, buckwheat, bulgar wheat, oatmeal and brown rice
» Nuts and seeds
» Tofu

VITAMIN C
» Citrus fruits
» Strawberries
» Kiwi fruit
» Peppers
» Broccoli
» Brussels sprouts
» Leafy greens
» Cauliflower
» Tomatoes
» Some herbs, including coriander, parsley, basil, thyme and chives

OMEGA 3
» Flaxseeds
» Chia seeds
» Hemp seeds
» Walnuts
» Seaweed, including nori, spirulina and chlorella
» Cauliflower
» Leafy greens
» Berries
» Mangoes
» Herbs and spices, including cloves, star anise, oregano and tarragon

B12
» Fortified foods including plant milks (not homemade), yogurts and cereal
» Nutritional yeast (also referred to as 'nooch', this is a cheesy powder that adds flavour to dishes, as well as boosting your B12)
» Marmite or other yeast extracts
» Chlorella

As you can see, there is a huge amount of crossover between the foods listed and the nutrients they each possess, making it easy for you to give your body everything it needs to thrive. I do have my blood work taken each year just to keep tabs on my overall levels, and I always ensure to supplement my B12 intake with an additional vitamin, which I take several times a week.

I'm not super organised and I don't plan my meals in advance because the spontaneity of creating something new (usually with limited ingredients) is half the fun. But, for those of you who do like a little more structure in your lives, hopefully this book will help … even if it's just a jumping off platform to get those ideas flowing. To make things super easy for you, I've included a suggested meal plan for one week on page 13 – just so you can see how simple turning vegan can be.

I don't limit myself in any way when it comes to grains, nuts, fruits or the like, nor do I shun whole food groups because they currently aren't 'in', because I trust my body to tell me when it's had enough (or, indeed, when it needs something) and that's when I might shake things up a bit. I haven't been on a diet since my twenties and I never partake in cleanses – they just make me miserable and I'm all about consistency, not fads. Granted, it's not a system without flaws but because I eat for pleasure, as much as anything else, I wouldn't dream of eliminating coffee, alcohol or sugar completely from my diet because, in small, occasional doses, they bring me immense happiness – a cold (vegan friendly) cider and packet of crisps at the pub is something I'm just not willing to give up. This is a balance that works for me, however, should these things send you into a downward spiral of self-loathing, you have two options: give them up entirely, or be a little less hard on yourself. I know which one I'd choose.

Perfection is something that is now endlessly linked with lifestyle and diet, so much so, we've become a western nation bordering on the 'orthorexic'. That is to say, we examine every morsel that passes our lips with decisions being made on how much nutritional value it has rather than how good it tastes. We should be considering both. If we look at some of

the healthiest nations in the world (certain parts of China, Japan and the Mediterranean) they've had this two-pronged attack of health and flavour nailed down for millennia. Living off the land, eating seasonally and locally, eschewing processed foods and having a gentle approach to their surroundings is the optimum way to feed body and soul, but with many of us now crammed into overpopulated cities, veganism is a terrific way to feed into this philosophy without having to flee to the country.

Above all else, it's crucial to note that everybody's balance and indeed 'wellness' barometer will be different. Just as life isn't a 'one size fits all' experience, nor will any two vegan journeys be the same. Sharing is important, but comparing can be detrimental, so remember to be supportive of each other, and allow yourself to make mistakes or have the odd stumble, because nothing is ever straightforward. Take solace in the fact that none of us are perfect, so do the best you can – and be well.

WHAT CAN YOU EAT?

When we first make the switch to veganism, our thoughts turn immediately to all the favourite foods we can no longer eat, whether it be cheese, steak or ice cream. It's a process that we all go through, because it takes time to let go of these foods and move forward into a brighter, plant-based, wholefoods future. Saying goodbye to these foods can leave you vulnerable to cravings that may weaken your vegan resolve.

So, how do we satiate these built-in cravings that we've probably been nurturing our entire lives? Well, the answer is quite simple really. Instead of looking back forlornly at all the cheeseburgers we've enjoyed over the years, we endeavour to move forward with a whole arsenal of new, exciting whole foods that will nourish our minds, bodies and souls. It's a truly exciting time, one where you will learn about delicious foods that you never even knew existed, as well as useful new cooking techniques that will elevate your kitchen status no end. It's also the start of you making the connection between what you put into your body and what it gives you in return, from energy and glowing skin to a more positive mindset.

To deal with these cravings and retrain your brain (and taste buds) to crave other foods, I suggest making a weekly menu. It's a proactive step towards fully integrating veganism into your busy life. Fear not, it will soon become second nature. Divide your menu into the necessary sections – breakfast, lunch, dinner and snacks. Getting a few simple dishes under your belt is crucial at the start, as it will ensure you are less likely to falter. But before I offer up a suggested meal plan, I would like to make a point that I really feel can't be stressed enough – this is NOT a diet. Yes, you are changing your 'dietary' lifestyle and these changes may have a positive effect on your health and weight, however, this should in no way

	BREAKFAST	LUNCH	DINNER	SNACKS/DESSERT
M	OVERNIGHT OATS page 29	ULTIMATE GRIDDLED SWEET POTATO SANDWICH page 63	BUTTON MUSHROOM AND CHICKPEA PIES page 94	BLISS BALLS pages 128-129
T	CHAI CHIA PARFAIT PUDDING page 31	CARROT AND COURGETTE TOSTADA page 56	GREEN LENTIL AND SPINACH CURRY page 76	CASHEW-COATED KALE CHIPS page 50
W	NO-BAKE GRANOLA BARS page 37	MUSHROOM AND TARRAGON SOUP page 74	ADUKI BEAN CASSEROLE page 119	APPLES WITH CARAMEL DIPPING SAUCE page 133
T	FIG AND GRAPEFRUIT GRANOLA page 32	SIMPLE NORI LUNCH WRAPS page 52	VIETNAMESE NOODLE BOWL page 88	SIMPLY OATY COOKIES page 154
F	SIMPLE BREAKFAST POLENTA page 34	KALE, APPLE AND FENNEL SALAD page 103	ROASTED TOMATO SOUP WITH ROSEMARY SALAD POTATOES page 75	ROSEMARY-COATED CASHEWS page 50
S	STOVE-TOP BEANS WITH A TWIST page 42	SCANDINAVIAN-STYLE OPEN SANDWICHES page 61	WALNUT MEAT TACOS page 96	BANOFFEE PIE page 153
S	BUCKWHEAT GRIDDLE-PAN WAFFLES page 36	BULGAR WHEAT BOWL page 91	SUPER GREEN SUNDAY NIGHT SPAGHETTI page 92	BEETROOT AND LEMON CUPCAKES page 144

be relied upon as a quick-fire way to shed the pounds or get fit. This meal plan is merely a tool that you can refer to in order to help you get started with your new lifestyle.

Once the fridge and cupboards are full of all this wondrous vegan-friendly fodder, you'll be less likely to be tempted back into your old ways. Get a batch of Bliss Balls (pages 128–129) immediately on the go for those times you need an instant sweet-fix, and take your time to really savour your meals in the evenings, allowing this new way of eating to overtake any lingering hankering after a hotdog. In the meal plan above, I've chosen a few of my favourite dishes from this book but you can replace them with simpler recipes if you are an inexperienced cook or haven't been terribly adventurous with your food choices in the past. That way you will ease your palate into this new way of eating and it hopefully won't be too much of a shock to the system.

EATING OUT

So that's your own kitchen sorted, but what about when you're out and about? Obvious swaps will come in the form of soya lattes (or whatever your coffee preference may be) but my top, top tip is to always be prepared. Whether you opt for homemade Bliss Balls or a bag of nuts, make sure you never leave home without provisions. That may sound extreme, but you will thank me later after you've wandered around for hours in search of a suitable snack only to remember that handy treat snaffled away in your bag. Equally, I like to carry a handful of herbal tea bags, just to be prepared.

If you're vegan already, you will no doubt be aware of the pitfalls of restaurant dining. But you will also know that it is improving all the time with big chains as well as smaller, independent outlets offering more and more vegan options. If your chosen restaurant has a vegan-friendly menu, hurrah! If not, fret not. There will

almost always be something on the menu that can be made to accommodate your needs. Asking questions will become par for the course and even though it might be embarrassing at first, a month in you won't even blink an eye.

Starters and dessert are often the trickiest courses but soup and sorbet are often a good choice. Obviously ask if either contains any dairy... randomly, sometimes establishments like to put egg-white in sorbet and we all know that butter and cream can feature heavily in soups. If you're at an Italian restaurant, bruschetta or minestrone are often good starter options, so long as they haven't tried to 'fancify' it by adding pesto, bacon or the like. Pizzas too are a good option. Load up on vegan-friendly toppings and tell them to hold the cheese (but go heavy on the sauce) and you've got yourself one seriously handsome dish to enjoy – oh, and did you know there are places in Italy that don't serve cheese on pizza anyway? See, you're not even missing out! Pasta arrabbiata is another favourite fallback of mine when eating out. Again, just ask a few straightforward questions to be sure it is indeed 'vegan friendly' and you should be good to go.

Different cuisines will present different problems, especially when it comes to the main course. I often find British food the trickiest as it is very meat-centric. Even if there happens to be a vegetarian dish on the menu, it's often slathered in cheese. However, I find I can always cobble together something, such as a baked potato with either beans or salad, and (as long as they haven't been tossed in butter) I always order a side of mixed vegetables too. Luckily, most places are beginning to expand their veggie offering and I regularly find that the veggie chilli is a suitable option (make sure they don't dollop on the soured cream though). A big bowl of that with a slice of chunky bread and I'm one happy girl.

If I want a blow-out dinner, however, I tend to opt for Indian, Chinese or Thai. So many of their dishes are vegan anyway, I find that I am often spoilt for choice. From massaman curries and rice noodle stir-fries to deep-fried tofu and potato-stuffed masala dosas, the list goes on and on – there's a veritable vegan feast to be had, as long as you know where to look.

There are less obvious ingredients too that you might want to keep a look out for. For example, make sure to ask if soups contain vegan-friendly stock... bafflingly some places like to use chicken stock in vegetable broths so it's definitely worth checking. Also, ask if the salad dressings contain any honey or egg (they sometimes use it in emulsified dressings). If you (or they) are unsure, simply ask for some olive oil and balsamic vinegar so you can dress the salad yourself.

I know, I know. This all sounds like a terrible faff and I'm not going to sugar-coat it, because in the beginning it will be one. Like I said though, after the usual adjusting period, all these questions will trip off the tongue and your brain will go into vegan auto-pilot. From my perspective though, it's imperative to not stress too much over the minutiae. Because, unless you are standing in the kitchen yourself, ensuring the chef is (a) using a completely different surface to prepare your food and (b) remembering to omit every single animal product that would otherwise be in the dish, you will never be 100 percent sure what is in your food... unless you are dining at a vegan-specific restaurant, and those, unfortunately, are few and far between. In my opinion, there are certain things you need to let slide unless you want to spend your days pushing away plates of perfectly good 'vegan' food just because you suspect an egg came within 10cm of it.

In the past, I've been served a vegan wrap that came with an unrequested side of coleslaw. Obviously, it was an oversight on their part given the fact I stated that I was vegan, but I was happy to scoop it off my plate, wipe the faint smear of mayonnaise from the side and eat the damn sandwich.

I could've sent it back (and in some cases I do) but I also hate the thought of a perfectly good vegan-friendly wrap going straight in the bin just because it brushed against some mayo. That was my call and maybe you would've made a different one – and truthfully, both responses are equally valid – but my point is, don't sweat the small stuff and get on with your life.

A NOTE ON THE SYMBOLS IN THIS BOOK:
Throughout the book, you'll see a couple of symbols used to highlight whether certain recipes are raw and/or gluten-free.

GLUTEN FREE   RAW

WHAT DO YOU TELL PEOPLE?

Ever heard the joke:
'How do you know if a
vegan's in the room?'
'Don't worry, they'll tell you.'
Um. Yeah. Basically guys, we vegans have
got a bit of a bad rap over the years for
being, shall we say, a wee bit vocal about
our chosen lifestyle.

The general public probably do have somewhat of a misconstrued notion that we love to shout it from the rooftops... 'I'M VEGAN!!', and in case you didn't hear the first time, 'I DON'T EAT, WEAR OR CONSUME ANY ANIMAL PRODUCTS!' Like I said, our collective image has been tarnished. Well, I'm definitely not a rooftop shouter, nor do I like telling people about my veganism, so you could say my behaviour is quite the opposite to that of a 'typical' (or should that be 'stereotypical') vegan. In fact, I cringe when my mother feels the need to inform the room that HER DAUGHTER IS A VEGAN! So, I guess that means I have a designated rooftop shouter doing all the shouting for me. Saves me the trouble I suppose.

Seriously, what you tell people is entirely up to you – but here are a few pointers I've learnt along the way that might come in handy. Some of you may disagree with my (gentle) tactics but my way of dealing with things is to always put myself in the other person's shoes – and to also remind myself of my pre-vegan days. Here are a few of my thoughts.

Don't be the first to bring it up because, in most instances, it won't come up naturally in the conversation anyway. In my experience, parties are for partying, not for forcing your agenda on some unsuspecting schmuck. The likelihood of you 'converting' whoever you may be chatting to is slim, and they're probably going to come away from the situation thinking, 'sheesh, those vegans are an intense lot', thus confirming every previous notion they may have had. That's not to say there's never a good time for the 'vegan' talk, but gauge it wisely because timing is everything. And no one wants to be lumbered with the ins and outs of your plant-based lifestyle at 1am after you've had a few beers. Trust me.

When you're out for dinner with friends, there may well be an awkward moment when you have to inform the waiter that you are, in fact, a vegan and therefore require a list of all their vegan options. This is never a straightforward scenario but it does get a little easier with time. At the beginning of my vegan journey going out to eat was painful, when the table would suddenly turn to you and almost collectively say, 'You're vegan?!' The polite thing to do is nod and hope you got away with it but no, wait for it... here come the questions! Ah, the questions – seemingly endless,

15

sometimes curious, occasionally aghast, mostly, always defensive! I think I've just about endured every reaction to my vegan status so I like to think I know a thing or two when it comes to dealing with them, so here's what I do.

Now, I realise it's very easy for me to say 'take it in your stride' but really that's what you've got to do. Otherwise, you're going to spend your days getting your knickers in a twist over someone else's opinion on your lifestyle choices. I understand your instant reaction might be to relate every gruesome slaughterhouse horror story you have heard, but believe me when I tell you this is only going to make an already uncomfortable situation ten times worse. If you do choose the 'shock' path, no one is going to come out of this conversation a happier person, least of all you. Most likely you will walk away feeling frustrated, belittled and vilified because confrontation is, quite frankly, a bummer. It has its place, of course, but I usually find that an evening out generally isn't it.

Passion, on the other hand, is great. Know your stuff, and if the probing is forceful, you can calmly lay out a few straightforward facts in a calm, reassuring 'I am totally not about to blow a gasket' tone. I also like to explain that non-vegan's lifestyle choices in no way offend me and, as I'm not making any judgement on them, I would kindly ask the same in return.

Then there are other times when I'm really, really, not in the mood to talk about veganism. Like, really. There is more to me than my dietary habits, so why can't we just talk about music and films already? I'm a human being and sometimes I just want to kick my shoes off, enjoy a glass of (vegan-friendly) wine and chill. In those instances, I rely on humour. Being casual, brushing something off and generally having a *laissez-faire* demeanour goes a long way to debunking those vegan myths and also gets the inquisitors of this world off your back. I've even had the gumption, on occasion, to say, 'I really don't want to talk about veganism tonight'. Cuts right to the chase and you can then get on with your evening without enduring the Spanish Inquisition or the glib remarks.

Obviously, my veganism is an integral part of who I am, but it's not everything and you shouldn't let it become your defining factor either, otherwise

it can easily consume your life. People frequently liken veganism to a religious cult and in some cases it's easy to see why when you consider the process... we become 'enlightened' (cue choirs of angels) and then 'want to spread the good word' ('Do you know what's actually in that nugget?!'). And I get it, I really do. I was practically giddy when I first decided to go down the vegan route. I couldn't wait to tell others of my new-found 'truth'. It was like I had stumbled upon the answer to the world's problems. I look back and realise that while my intentions were good, I probably overdid it. Anyway, my advice is not to 'NEVER TALK ABOUT YOUR VEGANISM' but to judge each situation and person on an individual basis. If someone is genuinely curious, there is a productive conversation to be had. If, however, you are confronted with someone who is simply trying to pick holes in your lifestyle, it really is best to take the high road. That's my tuppence worth and I'm sticking to it.

Even if you find it fairly easy to explain your veganism to your friends, you may find that your family are the tougher nuts to crack. Would you like me to tell you why? Announcing that you are now vegan is tantamount to saying they raised you wrong, fed you terribly and are just generally bad parents. They may take it as a direct slight and no matter how you sugar coat it, they could be offended. It's a natural reaction so expect lots of eye-rolls, tuts and comments such as 'it's only a phase'.

This is where patience comes in. It's an adjustment – both for you and your family. Yes, there might be a lot of questions, but be sure not to get ratty with anyone and, if you're pushed, simply explain your stance in a calm and reasonable manner. Lead by example and offer to cook an evening meal for everyone so they can see just how wonderful vegan food can be. This is your opportunity to make veganism inclusive rather than allowing it to divide the family. Make sure mealtimes aren't centred solely around 'vegan talk'. In fact, the less you talk about food at the table, the better, in my opinion. For me, the evening meal is a way to catch up on everyone's day – not a chance to 'convert' everyone at the dinner table. Keep the atmosphere casual and laidback – the less fraught your family feel about your decision, the more likely they are to view it favourably. And who knows, once they see how you are thriving (it will happen) they might eventually want to give it a go themselves.

If you happen to be the parent yourself and are trying to adjust your growing family's collective lifestyle, this could definitely get tricky. Depending on what age your children are and how cooperative your spouse is, there are several strategies you can utilise. Again, I would avoid announcing anything before or during a meal. Perhaps bring it up at a less food-focused time and explain that you think the family would benefit from 'veganising' their mealtimes with maybe a few reasons why – take your pick from health, welfare and the environment and go from there. If your kids are quite young, this will be way over their heads and all you'll be met with is blank stares and bewildered looks. In which case, you implement strategy number two, which is not to tell them at all. Simply make the necessary changes in the kitchen without any fuss and see if they even notice. Several meals in, drop the bombshell that they were eating vegan food all along and use that as your so-called 'way-in'. My own grandfather raves about my tea-making skills (and he is hard to please when it comes to tea!) and I've never once told him that he's actually drinking unsweetened soya milk.

Thankfully, there are now a number of children's books on the subject that help explain (in child-friendly terms) what veganism actually means. Order them online or ask your local bookseller to stock them, and don't be afraid to connect with other vegan families in the area. This is crucial so that your children don't feel like they're on their own or 'different' to everyone else. School is a delicate one to be handled with care, so above all else keep the fuss to a minimum. Inform your child's teacher and, if the school isn't in a position to provide a vegan alternative at snack time, pack a carton of plant milk and a vegan snack yourself so that your child won't feel left out.

I personally believe it is crucial not to force your child into doing something that makes them upset or uncomfortable. Only you know where you draw the line, but perhaps relinquishing control in some extreme cases may not be a bad thing – other kid's birthday parties, for example. After all, telling a child they can't have something only makes them want it more. Denying them a single cheese slice at a party may cause further problems down the line. Maintaining your vegan lifestyle within the home and throwing some kick-ass vegan birthday parties yourself will do more to win over your child than removing that tuna sandwich from their plate. In the long run they may well willingly choose a plant-based lifestyle but this might not happen if you force it upon them.

Above all, I am universally convinced that winning people over with food is the only surefire way to really get people on board this mighty vegan bandwagon – and, more importantly, to keep them there. Take it into your own hands, and instead of forcing Grandma to hear the hard truths about battery hens, let delicious, plant-based eats do all the talking for you. Because the one thing that people can't argue with is tasty, wholesome food. The rest, as they say, is up to you. Good luck!

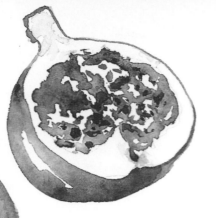

GOOD MORNINGS

BEETROOT *and* BANANA SMOOTHIE

I am very particular when it comes to smoothies, especially when they contain beetroot. The 'wow' colour (and blood pressure benefits) are undeniable, but beetroot can often render the flavour a little bit 'eww', so getting the balance right is crucial. Thankfully (and ever so smugly), I'm pleased to report that this smoothie possesses that exact balance. Thick enough to be a milkshake, this vibrant drink will change everything you ever thought (negative or otherwise) about beetroot in drinks – after all, those earthy overtones can be an acquired taste. If you remain unconvinced, reserve judgement until you sample the peculiarly purple delights for yourself. I'm certain you won't be disappointed. **Serves 1–2**

1 banana
50g pre-cooked vacuum-packed beetroot
2 stoned Medjool dates
180ml Plant Milk (see page 28); cashew is best
1 heaped teaspoon maca powder
handful of ice cubes (optional)

Put everything in a blender and blitz until completely smooth, scraping down the sides periodically. Serve in a tall glass with a straw.

NOTE: Maca is a root grown in Peru, and is usually found in powdered form. It has a slightly malty quality (making it a perfect addition to vegan shakes) and boasts a plethora of nutritional benefits, including calcium, zinc, iron, and those elusive B vitamins, too.

JUICES *without* a JUICER

Not got a juicer? No problem. Simply get yourself a nut milk bag or muslin cloth, and squeeze, squeeze, squeeze. I tend to err on the veggie side with my juices, adding just a smidge of necessary sweetness. They are so refreshing first thing, especially served in small tumblers with breakfast... they're such an intense hit, they'll be sure to give you that morning kickstart most of us need. The best thing about these particular juices is the balance. Even if you don't think you will like a juice crammed full of spinach, I have a feeling these subtle mixes might just change your mind. Feel free to experiment and find the combinations you like best.

Each serves 1–2

GREEN MONSTER

1 celery stick, roughly chopped
⅓ cucumber, peeled and chopped
handful of spinach
½ apple, chopped
1 passion fruit, pulp and seeds scooped out
1 tablespoon hemp powder (optional; available at health stores)
400ml filtered water

BUGS BUNNY

2 carrots, roughly chopped
1 apple, chopped
thumb-size piece of fresh ginger, peeled
500ml filtered water

VIRGIN BLOODY MARY

6 cherry tomatoes
1 small celery stick, roughly chopped
½ red chilli, deseeded
½ lemon, peeled
freshly ground black pepper
200ml filtered water

Put all the ingredients for your chosen juice in a high speed blender and blitz until smooth. Transfer to a nut milk bag and squeeze the juice into a bowl. Drink immediately.

TIP: Don't throw away the leftover pulp in the nut milk bag, save it for DIY beauty products, sauces, soups and bliss balls – nothing goes to waste here.

COCONUT, MANGO *and* SPINACH SMOOTHIE BOWL

Smoothie bowls are all the rage right now, and with good reason. The texture is ever so slightly thicker than your usual smoothie and the toppings add an extra dimension. If you're a total 'green smoothie' novice, this is possibly the best recipe to ease you in because, first and foremost, you can't taste the spinach at all. Not one tiny bit. Here, you're getting all the benefits without the aftertaste and, trust me, after one of these you'll be zipping around like nobody's business and feeling fit as a fiddle. Packed full of good fats, such as coconut oil and yogurt, which aid weight loss in the long run (they are known to decrease hunger and increase energy levels), you'll soon be hooked on their clean-eating credentials that'll have you glowing from the inside out. So swap that straw for a spoon and dig in. **Serves 1–2**

200g frozen mango chunks
½ ripe avocado, peeled
2 heaped tablespoons coconut yogurt
1 heaped teaspoon coconut oil
2 stoned Medjool dates
50g spinach leaves
juice of ½ lime
1 teaspoon spirulina/chorella or hemp powder
100ml Plant Milk (see page 28)
blueberries, fresh mango slices, flaked almonds
    and desiccated coconut, to serve

1. Place the frozen mango pieces in a food processor or blender along with the avocado, coconut yogurt, coconut oil, dates, spinach leaves, lime juice, spirulina and plant milk of your choice.
2. Blitz until completely smooth and serve in a shallow bowl with the fresh mango, a handful of fresh blueberries and a sprinkling of flaked almonds and desiccated coconut.

COOKIE DOUGH BALLS

CASHEW & MAPLE

APPLE PIE BALLS

PLANT MILK

Plant milk is a mainstay in pretty much every vegan's kitchen, so it's really worth investing in a nut milk bag. They are super cheap and you will use them all the time, especially when you realise just how easy and cheap making your own milk is. The general ratio I adhere to is one part nuts/oats to two parts water. This will render a smooth milk that isn't too thick or too thin ... and it keeps really well in the fridge. I like to soak my nuts beforehand, for at least 6 hours but preferably overnight. It renders the milk just that teeny bit creamier, but if you really don't have time unsoaked nuts will do just fine. Don't throw away that precious pulp either. Keep it for DIY beauty recipes (oat pulp makes for a particularly good facial scrub –see page 165) but perhaps more importantly, it is quite wondrous in bliss balls too. Overleaf, I've given some examples of how I like to 'pimp my milk' and make my bliss balls as yummy as possible. However, it's all up for grabs, as they say, so roll up your sleeves and get busy.

ALMOND & VANILLA

HAZELNUT & COCOA

OAT & CINNAMON

PLANT MILK 101

RAW · GLUTEN FREE

Serves 2–4 (makes about 500ml)

1 cup (about 110g) soaked nuts (almonds, cashews, hazelnuts or pistachios) or oats
2 cups (about 500ml) water (preferably filtered)

1. Place the soaked nuts or the oats in a blender along with the water and blend until it turns milky. If making oat milk, try not to over-blend the oats as it will impair the texture.

2. Strain the blended mixture through a sieve or pour into a nut milk bag set over a bowl and squeeze out all the liquid until only pulp remains in the bag. Set the pulp aside to make into bliss balls later. The milk is best fresh, but will keep in the fridge for 3–4 days.

'PIMP MY MILK'

Most of the time I like to keep things simple and *au naturel*. Now and again though, it's nice to add a little something – here are a few of my favourite combinations.

ALMOND & VANILLA

Simply scrape a vanilla pod into the almond milk before blending and straining (otherwise you'll end up with a milk dotted with seeds), and sweeten with a touch of agave nectar or maple syrup – although the sweetener is entirely optional, as it tastes just as lovely without.

CASHEW & MAPLE

Add 2 tablespoons maple syrup to the cashew milk, after it has been blended and sieved. Give it a quick whizz in the blender and serve over ice.

OAT & CINNAMON

One of my favourite combinations, this drink tastes pretty similar to a cool Mexican-style horchata – add the cinnamon (around a heaped teaspoon should do it) before blending and sweeten with agave nectar to taste. If you'd prefer not to use ground cinnamon, you could always add half a cinnamon stick prior to blending and sieving for the same effect.

HAZELNUT & COCOA

An absolute classic combination and one that will satisfy those latent childhood chocolate milk cravings – simply add 2 tablespoons of cocoa or cacao powder (plus a large stoned Medjool date or 1 tablespoon agave nectar) and a pinch of salt to the mix before blending and strain through the nut milk bag as normal.

'WASTE NOT, WANT NOT' BLISS BALLS

APPLE PIE BALLS

Combine the leftover almond pulp with 1 grated apple (remember to squeeze out any excess juice), a few stoned Medjool dates and 1 teaspoon ground cinnamon. Blend until it forms a squidgy rubble, then turn out onto a clean cutting board and form into balls. Roll each ball in ground cinnamon before chilling in the fridge for at least 1 hour but ideally overnight.

COOKIE DOUGH BALLS

Combine the remaining cashew and oat pulp with ½ tablespoon coconut oil, 2 tablespoons maple syrup (or agave nectar) and 30g ground almonds in a blender until it forms a squidgy rubble. Turn out onto a clean chopping board and work in a handful of chocolate chips. Form into balls before chilling in the fridge for at least 1 hour but ideally overnight.

NUTELLA BALLS

Blend the remaining hazelnut pulp with 1 tablespoon cocoa or cacao powder, 3–4 stoned Medjool dates and a generous pinch of salt until sticky. Turn out onto a clean cutting board, form into balls and roll in cocoa powder before chilling in the fridge for at least 1 hour but ideally overnight.

MIX-and-MATCH OVERNIGHT OATS

This is a one-size fits all recipe that frees you up to add whatever filling/topping/garnish you might fancy. I usually soak a batch of oats at the beginning of the week, which means I have breakfast sorted for three days running. I leave all the finessing until the next day, but you could easily make a complete bowl ahead of time. The base I use for all my overnight oats is equal parts oats to milk. This will sufficiently soak the oats and means you can then add any additional liquid should you wish. **Each bowl serves 1**

CARROT CAKE OATMEAL

25g oats
60ml Plant Milk (see page 28)
1 carrot, finely grated
1 teaspoon ground cinnamon
pinch of freshly grated nutmeg
juice of ½ orange
½ tablespoon maple syrup
1 tablespoon chopped walnuts
handful of raisins
½ tablespoon ground flaxseed

Soak the oats in the milk overnight. The next day, add the carrot to the bowl along with the cinnamon and nutmeg. Stir thoroughly before pouring in the orange juice and maple syrup. Stir through the nuts and raisins, and serve with a smattering of ground flaxseed.

NUTTY CHOCOLATE BOWL

25g oats
60ml Plant Milk (see page 28)
1 tablespoon cacao or cocoa powder
1 heaped tablespoon nut butter (almond, peanut, hazelnut or cashew)
½ tablespoon maple syrup
½ pear, sliced
1 tablespoon roughly chopped hazelnuts

Soak the oats in the milk overnight. The next day, add the cacao powder, nut butter, maple syrup and thoroughly combine. Serve with the sliced pear and roughly chopped hazelnuts.

TIP: This bowl also tastes delicious when combined with a mashed banana.

TROPICAL OATS

25g oats
60ml Plant Milk (see page 28)
¼ small pineapple
juice of ½ lime
½ tablespoon agave nectar
1 heaped tablespoon chopped mango
1 kiwi, peeled and sliced
½ banana, sliced
toasted desiccated coconut, to top

Soak the oats in the milk overnight. The next day, blitz the pineapple to a purée in a food processor or blender and add it to the oats along with the lime juice and agave. Stir to combine. Serve with the mango, kiwi, banana and some toasted coconut.

CHAI CHIA PARFAIT PUDDING

Chia seeds are having a moment and it's not difficult to see why. With a bounty of goodness that ranges from omega-3 through to protein and fibre, there are very few foods that can match their mighty status on the nutritional food front. Despite their miniature form, there's no better way to start the day especially when layered with a simple fruit soft serve that can be made in seconds – never mind breakfast, this could easily be dessert! **Serves 2**

2 bananas
240ml Plant Milk (see page 28)
4 finely ground cardamom seeds
¼ teaspoon ground cinnamon
good pinch of freshly ground nutmeg
1 heaped tablespoon agave nectar
40g chia seeds
75g frozen mixed berries, plus extra to serve
1 tablespoon agave nectar (optional)

1. Peel and chop the bananas and place them in the freezer for 24 hours.
2. Place the plant milk in a blender, along with the cardamom seeds, cinnamon, nutmeg and agave and blitz until combined.
3. Stir through the chia seeds until combined, transfer to a bowl, cover and refrigerate overnight.
4. The next day, place the frozen bananas, frozen berries and agave, if using, in a food processor or blender and blend until smooth and creamy.
5. Layer the chia pudding and soft serve into two glasses, topping each with frozen berries.

FIG *and* GRAPEFRUIT GRANOLA

Sugar is a hot topic right now and rightly so. While I'm not afraid of using refined sugar from time to time, day-to-day I try my best to limit my intake. Of course, maple syrup and agave nectar are sugars in themselves but the way I see it, the four meagre tablespoons used here will have been dispersed among eight servings of granola, and I can at least attest the sugar inclusion is as minimal as it could be without (crucially) impacting the taste, crunch or moreish quality of this zingy granola. My favourite way to serve it is to sprinkle a couple of heaped tablespoons of granola over some coconut yogurt and grapefruit segments – the citrus on citrus combo really helps set me up for the day. How will you eat yours? **Serves 8–10**

100g oats
1 teaspoon ground ginger
grated zest of 1 lemon
1 tablespoon coconut oil
juice of ½ grapefruit
4 tablespoons agave nectar or maple syrup
50g hazelnuts
30g pistachios
30g mixed seeds (such as pumpkin or sunflower)
100g dried figs

1. Preheat the oven to 160°C/gas mark 3.
2. Place the oats, ginger and lemon zest in a baking tray, stir to combine and gently toast in the oven for about 10 minutes.
3. Meanwhile, melt the coconut oil in a small saucepan before whisking in the grapefruit juice and the agave or maple syrup until combined.
4. Crush the hazelnuts and pistachios in a pestle and mortar (leaving a few whole) and set aside. Pulverise the seeds in a pestle and mortar or mini food processor and roughly chop the figs. Stir everything through the toasted oats until fully combined.
5. Pour over the syrup mix and coat thoroughly. Spread the mixture out on a large baking tray and bake for 40–45 minutes, shaking every 10 minutes to prevent sticking. Remove from the oven and leave to cool completely before transferring to a storage jar. The granola will keep for about a fortnight.

STUFFED BAKED APPLES *with an* ALMOND POURING CREAM

If you're anything like me, you'll welcome the chance to shake up your breakfast routine now and again just to keep things interesting. Chock-full of goodness, these simple baked apples are so sweet and soft they could almost be dessert. Pudding for breakfast you say? Count me in. **Serves 2**

½ tablespoon coconut oil, plus extra
   for greasing
2 apples
1 tablespoon oats
1 tablespoon ground almonds
1 tablespoon flaxseed
1 teaspoon ground cinnamon, plus
   extra for sprinkling
handful of raisins
3 tablespoons maple syrup

FOR THE ALMOND CREAM:
100g blanched almonds
300ml filtered water, plus extra
   for soaking
1 teaspoon vanilla extract
1 tablespoon agave nectar
pinch of salt

1. Firstly, soak the almonds for the almond cream. Cover the almonds with some filtered water and soak for at least 6 hours. Drain, rinse and set aside until needed.
2. Preheat the oven to 180°C/gas mark 4 and grease a baking dish with a little coconut oil.
3. Cut the tops off the apples (reserving both for later) and hollow out most of the insides using a spoon – make sure you leave enough flesh around the edges for the apple to maintain its shape when baked. Reserve the flesh for smoothies.
4. Mix the oats, ground almonds, flaxseed, coconut oil, raisins and cinnamon in a separate bowl to form a rough crumble. Use it to fill each apple and place them in the baking dish. Place the tops back on the apples, drizzle with maple syrup and a little more cinnamon and bake for 45–50 minutes until the apples are soft and the crumble topping is nicely golden.
5. While the apples are baking, put the soaked almonds, 300ml fresh filtered water, the vanilla, agave and salt in a food processor or blender and blitz until smooth and a pourable consistency – you may have to scrape down the sides several times to ensure there are no lumps. Refrigerate until needed.
6. Remove the baked apples from the oven and serve hot with the almond cream.

SIMPLE BREAKFAST POLENTA *with* ROSE-ROASTED PLUMS

I know we don't often associate polenta with sweetness or indeed 'breakfast' but this fine, naturally gluten-free grain is a wonderful option if you are tired of porridge. I sweeten mine with agave, but you could use any other vegan sweetener. If you've got time, these rose-roasted plums are a wonderful accompaniment to your polenta. Add a few crushed seeds, a final drizzle of plum syrup and maybe even an additional splash of plant milk and you're officially good to go – rise and shine, your perfect breakfast bowl awaits! **Serves 2–3**

400ml filtered water
50g polenta
50ml Plant Milk (see page 28)
2 tablespoons agave nectar
1 teaspoon vanilla extract
crushed pistachios, to serve

FOR THE PLUMS:
3 plums, halved and stoned
½ teaspoon allspice
pinch of sumac (optional)
1 tablespoon rose water
4 tablespoons agave nectar or maple syrup
1 heaped tablespoon palm or brown sugar
1 tablespoon pomegranate molasses
2 star anise
1 small stick of cinnamon

1. For the plums, preheat the oven to 180°C/gas mark 4. Place the plums flesh side up in a roasting dish and sprinkle over the allspice, sumac, rose water, agave or maple syrup, sugar and pomegranate molasses. Place the star anise and cinnamon in the dish along with a splash of water to prevent sticking. Roast for 30 minutes or until the plums are soft, juicy and gooey. Cool and refrigerate until needed.

2. Now, make the polenta. Bring the water to the boil in a saucepan and whisk in the polenta. Reduce the heat immediately to a very gentle simmer and keep whisking until it thickens.

3. Once thickened, add the Plant Milk, agave and vanilla and whisk until it fully amalgamates. Simmer for several minutes until it turns thick and creamy, whisking occasionally to prevent any lumps from forming. Divide between two bowls and top each with roasted plums and crushed pistachios.

BUCKWHEAT GRIDDLE-PAN WAFFLES

From pancakes to oats and even a full-on vegan fry-up, breakfast has long been my favourite meal of the day. But, not being one for gadgets, I often thought a waffle iron was just an expense too far and so waffles remained off limits... that is, until now. I'd always known griddle pans were wondrous things but I didn't appreciate their full worth until I attempted rustling up a 'griddle pan waffle'. Long story short, I was instantly sold and what you see here is the gluten-free result of my countless labours... if you find making and eating waffles 'laborious'. This is mildly groundbreaking territory, if (like me) you don't actually possess a waffle iron – I now have no intentions of acquiring one. **Serves 2–3 (makes 4–6 waffles, depending on size)**

TIP: For best results, ensure your griddle is extra clean to prevent any sticking.

100g buckwheat flour
½ teaspoon (gluten-free) baking powder
pinch of salt
125ml Plant Milk (see page 28)
½ tablespoon vanilla extract
2 tablespoons agave nectar or maple syrup
½ tablespoon melted coconut oil, plus extra for cooking

1. Lightly whisk the buckwheat flour, baking powder and salt together in a large bowl.
2. In a separate bowl or jug, vigorously whisk the milk, vanilla, agave or maple syrup and coconut oil together until fully combined and a little frothy.
3. Make a well in the centre of the flour, pour in the wet ingredients and fold gently, being careful not to overwork the mixture.
4. Heat a ridged griddle pan over a medium heat, generously brush with coconut oil and ladle one-quarter of the mixture into the pan – it should naturally form a round shape. Once bubbles begin to appear on top and the edges crisp, loosen the waffle from the pan using a palette knife.
5. When it is golden and marked, it is time to flip – to ensure it is equally crispy on the other side, brush it with a little more oil before flipping. I also like to press the waffle down firmly using a plate to ensure the batter gets into all the ridges of the pan and becomes super crispy.
6. Serve hot with a handful of blueberries, lightly whipped coconut cream and a decent drizzle of maple syrup.

NO-BAKE GRANOLA BARS

I'm all about ease in the kitchen. When something becomes too much of a faff I tend to look for shortcuts that won't diminish the overall dish. In this case, the faff too far is the baking bit, which is exactly why I've sidestepped this part and gone straight for a refrigerated version that tastes just as good, if not better! Packed full of nuts, seeds and dried fruit, these no-bake granola bars are just the thing for busy mornings (or mid-afternoon pick-me-ups) and go particularly well with a steaming mug of tea. **Makes 10 bars**

TIP: Melt some dark chocolate chips and drizzle over the top before cutting. Refrigerate for another 30 minutes before serving.

150g oats
½ tablespoon maca powder (optional; see note on page 20)
30g almonds, roughly chopped
30g sunflower seeds
30g pumpkin seeds
30g raisins
2 large stoned Medjool dates, chopped
30g desiccated coconut
30g dark chocolate chips
1 ripe banana
4 tablespoons coconut oil, melted
3 tablespoons peanut butter
2 tablespoons cashew or almond butter (available at most supermarkets)
1 teaspoon vanilla extract
5 tablespoons agave nectar
pinch of salt

1. Mix all the dry ingredients together in a bowl.
2. Mash the banana and whisk in the melted coconut oil, nut butters, vanilla and agave until completely smooth. Pour over the granola mix and stir to combine.
3. Line a brownie tin with baking parchment and tip the sticky granola mix into it, flattening to the edges with the back of a spoon or spatula. Refrigerate for at least 1 hour. Cut lengthways into long bars, then halve each one – you should get about 10 bars from each batch.

BUCKWHEAT BREAKFAST MUFFINS

Being prepared for breakfast can take the stress out of mornings. If you spend a little too much time in the shower to make anything from scratch, these gluten-free muffins are the perfect 'rise-and-shine' option that will get your day off to a nutritious start. Date-sweetened, they are full of goodness and, more importantly, incredibly filling too. Buckwheat is such a wonderfully wholesome flour and really adds to the nubbly, nutty texture of these breakfast beauties. No more skipping breakfast for you! **Makes 6**

100g buckwheat flour

20g gold-milled flaxseed (linseed), plus extra for topping

20g ground almonds

10g chia seeds, plus extra for topping

¾ teaspoon (gluten-free) baking powder

¼ teaspoon bicarbonate of soda

4 stoned Medjool dates

1 tablespoon maple syrup, plus extra for brushing

1 banana

150ml Plant Milk (see page 28)

1 tablespoon chopped walnuts

1 tablespoon sunflower seeds, plus extra for topping

handful of raisins

1. Preheat the oven to 180°C/gas mark 4.

2. Whisk the flour, flaxseed, ground almonds, chia, baking powder and bicarbonate of soda together in a large bowl.

3. Blitz the dates with the maple syrup in a food processor or blender until it forms a thick paste.

4. Mash the banana to a purée and whisk together with the date paste and plant milk until smooth.

5. Make a well in the centre of the flour and add the wet mixture. Fold gently until thoroughly combined before stirring through the walnuts, sunflower seeds and raisins. Divide between six large muffin cases and bake for 20 minutes.

6. Remove from oven and brush the tops with maple syrup while still hot. Crush some flaxseed, chia and sunflower seeds in a pestle and mortar and garnish each muffin. Serve warm or store until needed. These are best eaten fresh, but will keep for a couple of days in an airtight container.

GLUTEN
FREE

FUSS-FREE
CHIA JAM

Let's be honest. Jam is a bit of
a pain to make. And I'll be the
first to admit I've ruined the odd
pan in the process – damn you
blackberries, damn you. But when
I started experimenting with
this chia seed alternative, it was
almost as if I'd stumbled upon the
holy grail of preserve making. So
embarrassingly simple is it to make,
I'm loath to even categorise it as a
recipe but nevertheless, here it is in
all its 2-minute construction glory.
Enjoy. **Makes 6–8 servings**

150g strawberries, washed and hulled
4 tablespoons vegan sweetener (such as
    agave nectar or maple syrup)
1 teaspoon lemon juice
1 tablespoon vanilla extract
3 tablespoons chia seeds

1. Put the strawberries in a small blender
with the sweetener, lemon juice and
vanilla. Blend to a runny purée, then strain
through a fine-mesh sieve.
2. Transfer to a bowl, stir through the chia
seeds and leave to set and thicken in the
fridge for at least 1 hour. Use on toast, in
puddings or as a jam substitute in a vegan
cream tea. This jam will keep in the fridge
for 5–7 days.

RAW
GLUTEN
FREE

COCONUT
BUTTER

This is probably the easiest recipe
you're likely to come across – the
only downside is the time it takes
to turn from shredded pieces of
coconut into a smooth runny
butter. Patience is paramount.
Persevere and you'll be left with
a rich, unctuous butter that has
a multitude of uses. Serve on hot
toast, stir it into smoothies, or use
it as a dip with fruit, a great topping
for cupcakes, or as a filling for
raw desserts – simply make a nut
casing, fill with coconut butter and
top with fresh fruit. **Makes 6–8 servings**

200g desiccated coconut

Place the coconut in a food processor or
blender and blend for about 10–15 minutes
until smooth and runny, scraping down
the sides from time to time. Transfer to a
sterilised jar and store in a warm place.

NOTE: Coconut is very sensitive to
temperature so may return to a solid state
when stored. If this happens, simply place
the jar in a bowl of warm water until the
mixture loosens.

GOOD MORNINGS

EASY WHOLEMEAL LOAF

I'm not going to lie, bread is central to my very existence. Carbs, schmarbs – in my opinion, a world without toast is not a world worth living in. Perhaps it's a nostalgia thing, but bread remains my ultimate fail-safe comfort food, rendering any disastrous day into a manageable one. With that said, shop-bought loaves have quickly become my nemesis. Full of preservatives, they leave me feeling unsatisfied and bloated rather than content and full, which is where this easy homemade wholemeal loaf steps in. Unlike other bread recipes that take a lot of tender-loving care, this is a knead-once, bung in the oven option that even the beginner baker can easily tackle... now that's music to my bread-lovin' ears. Best of all, it toasts beautifully, which means breakfast is officially sorted. **Serves 8–10**

400g wholemeal flour
275g plain white flour, plus extra for dusting
generous pinch of salt
pinch of sugar
7g (about 1½ teaspoons) fast-action dried yeast
350ml hand-hot water
2 tablespoons olive oil

1. Mix both the flours with the salt, sugar and yeast in a large bowl. Measure the water into a measuring jug and add the oil.
2. Pour half the liquid into the bowl and mix quickly to form a ball. Add the rest of the water gradually. Once you've formed a rough ball, stop adding the water. If it becomes too wet add more flour, although it should be a little tacky to the touch.
3. Flour a clean work surface and turn out the dough. Knead the dough for around 5 minutes until it is smooth, elastic and no longer sticky.
4. Grease a 1kg loaf tin with a smidge of oil or vegan margarine. Press or roll out the dough to the length of the tin, then stretch it to three times the width. Fold the long sides to the middle, turn over so the joins are underneath, then drop into the loaf tin. You can tuck the dough in if it doesn't fit perfectly. Cover with a clean tea towel and leave to rise in a warm place for 1 hour until doubled in size. You'll know it's ready when the dough springs back to the touch.
5. Preheat oven to 220°C/gas mark 7. Dust the loaf with flour for a soft crust or brush with Plant Milk (see page 28) for a shiny one. Bake for 30–35 minutes until golden. Turn out the loaf when warm – it should sound hollow when tapped on the bottom. Leave to cool on a wire rack.

STOVETOP BEANS
with a TWIST

I've got a confession to make. Baked beans (yup, the canned variety) are my weakness. They are my ultimate go-to convenience comfort food and the perfect thing to soothe a sore head, and even a sore heart. That said, I decided to come up with my own homemade version and this is the triumphant result. The slightly Asian base (the holy trinity as it were... garlic, chilli and ginger) is the crucial element in these beans. Whereas the shop-bought variety will be packed full of sugar and salt, this stovetop equivalent requires a mere splash of maple syrup (to help with the acidity) and minimal salt. The simmering of the sauce is paramount in getting the texture 'just so' before adding the haricot beans. I like to cook them until there is very little liquid left but if you prefer them slightly more 'saucy', add a touch more water. The taste intensifies the longer you leave the sauce, making this a great dish to make the day before – by the time you reheat the beans they will have absorbed all those wonderful flavours and spices. I'm all about toast in this instance but they would be equally great as part of a vegan fry-up or even on some brown rice for a hearty mid-week meal. **Serves 2–4**

1 tablespoon olive oil

3 garlic cloves

thumb-size piece of fresh ginger

1 small chilli, deseeded

400g can plum tomatoes

1 tablespoon tomato purée

½ tablespoon maple syrup

½ tablespoon balsamic vinegar

1 heaped teaspoon Marmite

splash of chilli sauce (Tabasco, Cholula etc.)

400g can haricot beans, drained and rinsed

sea salt and freshly ground black pepper

1. Heat the oil in a heavy-based saucepan. Finely mince the garlic, ginger and chilli together on a clean chopping board. Add it to the pan, along with a little salt and gently fry until the aromas begin to exude.

2. Pour in the plum tomatoes and break them up using the back of a spoon. Fill the empty tomato can half-full with water and swill the can to get any remaining juice before tipping it into the pan. Leave it to simmer for 10 minutes, by which stage the tomatoes will have softened further and you can crush it into a passata-like sauce.

3. Add the tomato purée and stir to combine before adding the maple syrup, balsamic vinegar, marmite and hot sauce. Season and simmer for around 45 minutes or until the sauce has reduced considerably.

4. Add the haricot beans to the pan, season and stir before simmering for a further 15–20 minutes.

5. Serve immediately on some hot sourdough toast or, alternatively, reheat the following day.

SAVOURY 'INDIAN-STYLE' CRÊPES

Wafer thin but with a good amount of chew, these are the ultimate grab-and-go pancakes. They are so easy you could happily make them a weekday feature – and best of all there's no flipping required, yippee! With a slight nod to India (I love my spices and can't get enough of gram flour) these have pretty much surpassed any existing savoury pancake recipe in my repertoire. I've gone for a butter bean filling because I wanted to keep this dish as straightforward as possible. Simplicity aside, the creaminess of the butter beans are the perfect pairing to the tangy crêpes and the spinach is that final green flourish I can't do without... although rocket would work just as well. **Serves 2–3**

50g gram flour
50g plain white flour
¼ teaspoon bicarbonate of soda
½ teaspoon sea salt
1 teaspoon ground turmeric
juice of ½ lemon
180ml water
½ tablespoon coconut oil, plus a little extra
   for oiling
spinach leaves, wilted or raw (optional)
hot sauce (Tabasco, Cholula etc.) (optional)

FOR THE 'BUTTER BEAN' FILLING:
400g can butter beans, drained and rinsed
¼ teaspoon sea salt
juice of ½ lemon
½ teaspoon garam masala

1. Roughly mash the butter beans with the salt, lemon juice and garam masala in a bowl and set aside.
2. Whisk both flours with the bicarbonate of soda, sea salt and turmeric in a bowl. Whisk in the lemon juice and water. Melt the coconut oil in a small heavy-based frying pan and add to the batter. Whisk to combine.
3. Return the pan to the heat and when it has reached a medium-high heat, add just under half a ladle of batter. Swirl the pan so the batter meets the edges and cook until you see bubbles appearing on top and the edges look crispy.
4. Place a layer of spinach leaves, if using, in the centre of the crêpe and add a tablespoon of the butter bean mixture and a splash of your favourite hot sauce, if using. Use a spatula to roll the crêpe.
5. Carefully remove the rolled crêpe from the pan and repeat. You can keep the crêpes warm in a low oven or consume hot straight out of the pan.

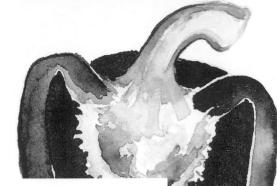

SNACKS *and* LUNCHES

GLUTEN FREE

VEGAN SNACKS

Yes, it's true, we vegans love to snack. However, instead of spending a fortune on the 'healthy' shop-bought vegan variety I prefer to make my own version in batches, keeping them on hand for whenever the mood strikes. Not only are they delicious, they happen to pack a punch in the nutritional department too – blackstrap molasses, which you can buy in health stores, is rich in iron, cashews are high in antioxidants and kale is basically a bona fide superfood that remains top of my fave foods list. Turn over for some of my favourite snack recipes.

CRUNCHY CHIPOTLE CHICKPEAS

Serves 2–4

200g canned chickpeas, drained and rinsed
1 tablespoon blackstrap molasses
1 tablespoon chipotle paste
1 tablespoon soy sauce
1 tablespoon olive oil
1 tablespoon agave nectar
1 teaspoon ground cumin
1 teaspoon smoked paprika
pinch of cayenne pepper

1. Preheat the oven to 180°C/gas mark 4.
2. Thoroughly dry the chickpeas in a clean tea towel until most of the skins have been removed, then transfer to a baking dish.
3. Whisk the rest of the ingredients together in a small bowl and pour over the chickpeas. Toss the chickpeas around in the marinade until coated, then roast for about 30–35 minutes, shaking the pan periodically. Leave to cool completely before eating.

CASHEW-COATED KALE CHIPS

Serves 2–4

100g kale, stalks removed and large pieces torn into smaller pieces

FOR THE CASHEW PASTE:
50g soaked cashews
juice of ½ lemon
1 tablespoon tamari or soy sauce (please note that if you choose soy sauce, this recipe will not be gluten-free)
2 teaspoons wasabi
1 teaspoon Dijon mustard
1 teaspoon cider vinegar

1. Preheat the oven to the lowest setting, 100°C/gas mark ¼.
2. Place the cashew paste ingredients into a small food processor or blender and blend until smooth. Rub the paste into the kale, then spread the kale out onto a large baking sheet – they may have to be baked in batches as you need them in a single layer.
3. Bake for about 1 hour 20 minutes until crispy. Leave to cool completely before eating.

ROSEMARY-COATED CASHEWS

Serves 2–4

1 tablespoon agave nectar
1 teaspoon olive oil
150g cashews
2 rosemary sprigs, leaves finely chopped
1 heaped teaspoon sea salt
2 heaped teaspoons sugar or crushed palm sugar

1. Preheat the oven to 175°C/gas mark 3–4 and line a baking tray with baking parchment.
2. Whisk the agave and oil together. Place the cashews in the baking tray, pour over the agave/oil mixture and toss to combine. Sprinkle over the rosemary and toss to coat.
3. Sprinkle generously with salt and sugar and roast for about 1 hour or until golden, shaking frequently to prevent burning or sticking.
4. Remove from the oven and generously sprinkle with more salt and sugar. Set aside to cool completely.

BAKED FALAFEL BURGERS

Like many vegans, falafel is my go-to savoury snack food but, by golly, they can be a pain to make. As they are prone to disintegrating when shallow fried, I decided to forgo the frying-pan palaver a long time ago and instead opt for a healthier, baked option. Crammed full of fragrant coriander with just the right touch of lemon, these fragrant burger-style patties are perfect in a pitta or atop a wholesome bulgar bowl tossed with roasted veggies (see page 91). Or why not form into smaller burger bites for an excellent canapé, adorned with a dollop of hummus and a slice of fig – these are endlessly versatile. **Serves 2–4**

TIP: For a crunchy exterior, toss these falafel burgers in sesame seeds before baking.

400g can chickpeas, drained and rinsed
25g fresh coriander
2 garlic cloves
2 spring onions
1 heaped teaspoon ground cumin
½ teaspoon smoked paprika
1 tablespoon plain flour
juice of ½ lemon
2 tablespoons olive oil
sea salt and freshly ground black pepper

1. Preheat the oven to 200°C/gas mark 6.
2. Put the chickpeas in a food processor or blender along with the coriander, garlic, spring onions, cumin, paprika, flour, lemon juice, oil and some seasoning. Pulse until it all comes together – it should be fairly coarse.
3. Tip the mixture out onto a plate or board and shape into 4 medium-size burger patties. Place on a baking tray.
4. Bake for 20 minutes before gently turning and baking for a further 20 minutes on the other side.
5. Serve in a freshly toasted pitta along with some salad leaves, tahini dressing, hummus and chilli sauce.

SIMPLE NORI LUNCH WRAPS

These simple seaweed wraps have become a bit of a lunchtime standard for me, and they're great for taking on picnics too. Possessing a multitude of impressive nutrients including protein, vitamin C, calcium and even omega 3s, nori is a little powerhouse of health that really should not be overlooked. While I'm a massive sushi fan, sometimes making it can feel like a bit of a faff... plus there's something so satisfying about biting into a burrito-style wrap – it's almost like tricking your brain into thinking it's bread! **Serves 2**

100g quinoa
1 avocado, peeled and stoned
juice of ½ lime
1 spring onion, finely chopped
1 small celery stick, finely chopped
30g fresh coriander, roughly chopped
2 nori sheets
spinach leaves, stalks removed (you will need about 5–6 leaves per roll)
1 carrot, peeled and finely sliced into strips
sea salt

FOR THE PASSION FRUIT SAUCE:
1 passion fruit
juice of ½ lime
½ teaspoon agave nectar

1. To make the passion fruit sauce, strain the insides of the passion fruit through a tea strainer or fine-mesh sieve to remove the seeds. Whisk the juice with the lime juice, agave and a pinch of salt in a small bowl and set aside.

2. To cook the quinoa, simply cover with twice the amount of water to grain in a saucepan, cover, bring to the boil, then reduce to a gentle simmer for about 20–25 minutes or until all the liquid has been absorbed. Set aside to cool.

3. Mash the avocado flesh with a little lime juice and salt.

4. Once the quinoa has cooled sufficiently, stir through half the mashed avocado, the spring onion, celery, coriander and some of the passion fruit sauce. Season with salt.

5. Place the nori sheets shiny side down. Spread a spoonful of the remaining avocado in the centre near the top edge of each sheet and layer over some spinach leaves. Divide the cooked quinoa between the nori sheets, ensuring not to overfill (you may have a little left over), drizzle over the remaining passion fruit sauce and top with the carrot strips.

6. To make the wrap, fold in both sides and gently but firmly roll into a burrito shape, brushing the ends with water to secure. Wet a sharp knife and cut each wrap at a diagonal. Serve alongside any remaining sauce.

QUESO-LESS QUESADILLA *with an* APPLE CHUTNEY

Once you've prepared the 'cheesy' spread and chutney, these queso-free quesadillas are an absolute cinch to make. If I know I'm going to have a busy week, I try to prepare a batch of both ahead of time, which means I can have a hot homemade lunch in minutes. I like to think of it as a ploughman's twist on a tortilla dish that has become something of a staple in my kitchen. **Serves 4**

4 large flour tortillas
1 batch of Easy Cashew Cheese
  Spread (see page 61)
handful of rocket
olive oil, for brushing

**FOR THE APPLE AND GINGER
CHUTNEY:**
1 tablespoon olive oil
1 small onion, finely diced
2 small eating apples, peeled, cored
  and sliced
1 tablespoon lemon juice
2 tablespoons red wine vinegar
3 tablespoons agave nectar
1 teaspoon sambal oelek or other
  chilli paste
handful of raisins or sultanas
thumb-size piece of fresh ginger,
  peeled and grated
salt

1. First, make the chutney. Heat the olive oil in a small saucepan and add the onion. Season with a little salt and sauté until translucent.

2. Toss the apple slices in a little lemon juice to prevent them discolouring. Add them to the pan along with the red wine vinegar, agave, sambal oelek, raisins or sultanas and grated ginger. Stir to combine, add a splash of water and simmer for around 20 minutes until most of the liquid has evaporated and the mixture is completely soft. Leave it to cool before transferring to a clean, sterilised jar. Refrigerate until needed.

3. Heat a griddle or frying pan and divide the Easy Cashew Cheese Spread between the four tortillas, spreading it in a half moon shape. Top with a tablespoon or so of the chutney and a smattering of rocket. Fold in half and brush each side with a little oil. Griddle over a medium heat until marked and golden on both sides. Cut each tortilla into three triangles and serve.

FRIED TOFU 'PO-BOY' BAGUETTE

Okay, so this is a bit of a palaver for a quick lunchtime dish but 'po-boy' is it worth the effort – see what I did there? Ahem. The panko-fried tofu is a thing of sheer magic that will convert even the most fervent bean curd naysayers, bringing a little creole crunch to this plant-based table of ours. The seasoning is just enough to lift the tofu out of the doldrums and if this easy soya mayo doesn't fool even a few of your friends, I'll happily eat my hat. All we need now is a cold beer – or a 'New Awlins' style cocktail – and we are officially good to go. **Serves 4**

TIP: To make the mayo 'spicy', simply stir through 1 heaped teaspoon harissa or chilli paste.

150g firm tofu
60g panko breadcrumbs
1 tablespoon plain flour
1 teaspoon paprika, plus extra to serve
½ teaspoon smoked paprika
½ teaspoon dried thyme
½ teaspoon dried oregano
pinch of cayenne pepper
2 tablespoons Dijon mustard
1 tablespoon lemon juice
olive oil, for frying
sea salt and freshly ground black pepper

FOR THE SOYA MAYO:
150g silken tofu
juice of ½ lemon
1 teaspoon Dijon mustard
1 teaspoon sea salt
75ml olive oil

TO SERVE:
1 large baguette
little gem lettuce
sliced radishes

1. Drain and rinse the tofu. Pat it dry and place in a shallow bowl. Put a plate on top, weight it down with several cans and set it aside for at least 1 hour. Once it has exuded all its excess liquid, drain again and refrigerate until needed, preferably overnight.

2. Blitz the panko breadcrumbs to a very fine rubble in a food processor. Transfer to a dish and combine with the flour, paprika, smoked paprika, thyme, oregano, cayenne and some seasoning.

3. Slice the tofu into even rectangular shapes about 1cm thick. Mix the mustard and lemon juice together, then brush onto each tofu piece until covered. Dredge thoroughly in the panko mix and set aside until needed.

4. Heat about 5mm oil in a small frying pan. Test the oil by dropping in some breadcrumbs – if they turn golden, it is at the correct temperature. A controlled medium heat is best.

5. Fry the tofu in batches of 2–3 at a time, turning until golden and crispy all over. Transfer to a plate and lightly season while still hot. Repeat with the remaining tofu.

6. For the mayo, place the silken tofu, lemon juice, mustard and salt in a food processor or blender. Blend until smooth before gradually adding the oil through the funnel until it has fully emulsified. Check for seasoning and refrigerate until needed. It won't be as thick as shop-bought mayo.

7. When you are ready to serve, gently heat the baguette before quartering. Halve each quarter and spread the bottom part with the soya mayo. Layer on the little gem lettuce leaves, a smidge more mayo, sliced radish and the panko-fried tofu. Mix a tablespoon or two of the mayo with 1 teaspoon paprika and spread on the other half of the baguette before sandwiching together. Serve.

CARROT *and* COURGETTE TOSTADA

Single serve dishes are my bag these days, especially when it comes to lunch. Although I dine alone most afternoons, I still want that full-on flavour experience... even when I only have minutes to spare. Thankfully, these crispy tostadas (basically a mini Mexican pizza) are just the ticket when I have very little time but still want something satisfying. The carrot and courgette ribbons aren't exactly authentic Mexican fare, so let's just say this is my anglicised twist on a Central American classic – not that I'm apologising, mind, because flavour is what counts here and, in my humble opinion, this super simple tostada tastes pretty darn good. **Serves 1**

HOW TO TOAST SEEDS

Toast pumpkin seeds (or seed of your choice) in a dry pan over a medium heat until they just begin to brown, making sure to toss them occasionally to prevent burning.

TIP: If you can't get your hands on a taco-size tortilla, you can always cut a regular one to size using a bowl. Simply place an upturned cereal bowl onto a soft flour or corn tortilla and carefully cut around it using a sharp knife – *et voilà*, the perfect taco tortilla.

1 tablespoon olive oil
1 garlic clove, finely sliced
1 small carrot, peeled into ribbons
½ courgette, peeled into ribbons
1 small taco tortilla (preferably stale)
1 tablespoon toasted pumpkin seeds, to garnish
sea salt and freshly ground black pepper

FOR THE AVOCADO SPREAD:
1 ripe avocado, peeled and stoned
juice of ½ lemon or lime
1 teaspoon Dijon mustard

1. Heat the olive oil in a small frying pan and add the garlic and a pinch of salt. Gently fry for a minute or two before adding the carrot and courgette ribbons. Gently sauté for several minutes until they just begin to soften – be sure not to cook them for too long, however, or you risk them losing their vibrancy and texture. Set aside until needed.
2. To make the avocado spread, mash the avocado with some salt and lemon or lime juice until smooth. Stir through the mustard and set aside until needed.
3. Heat a griddle pan to a high heat and brush the tortilla with the oil from the vegetable pan. Griddle each side until marked and crispy. Transfer to a plate and let it sit for a few minutes – if you add your toppings immediately, your tostada may turn soggy.
4. Spread the avocado all over the tostada before piling on the sautéed ribbons. Sprinkle over the toasted pumpkin seeds and serve.

CREAMY COURGETTE DIP *with* QUICK PRESERVED LEMONS

Coupled with my Quick Preserved Lemons, this courgette dip is the perfect pairing for any meze, adding a little touch of Middle-Eastern wow factor – and bringing with it a welcome break from the usual hummus offerings. Be cautious of over-seasoning, as the courgettes will absorb the salt and become bitter. Taste as you go along to achieve the right balance.

Serves 2–4

2 large courgettes, halved lengthways
olive oil, for drizzling
1 teaspoon cumin
1 teaspoon dried oregano
1 small garlic clove, grated
1 tablespoon lemon juice
3 tablespoons dairy-free yogurt (either soya or coconut)
1 tablespoon extra virgin olive oil
sea salt and freshly ground black pepper

1. Preheat the oven to 200°C/gas mark 6. Place the courgettes in a baking tray and drizzle with olive oil. Season, cover loosely with foil and roast for around an hour until soft, turning once.

2. Let the courgettes cool completely before scooping out the flesh. Transfer to a food processor along with the cumin, oregano, garlic, lemon juice and yogurt. While the ingredients are processing, drizzle in the extra virgin olive oil until the dip has emulsified and thickened. Check for seasoning and serve with a tablespoon or so of preserved lemons (see below) scattered on top.

FOR THE QUICK PRESERVED LEMONS:
2 large lemons, unwaxed, preferably organic
6 tablespoons agave nectar
2 heaped tablespoons salt

1. Wash and wipe the lemons before dicing them into small bite-size pieces. Place in a saucepan along with the agave and salt, and a splash of water.

2. Bring to the boil and then gently simmer for around 10–15 minutes to gently soften the lemon pieces. Transfer to a clean jar, screw on the lid and set aside to cool. These will keep for up to 1 week in a sealed jar in the fridge.

CHUNKY BUTTER BEAN DIP *with a* FRAGRANT BASIL OIL

Mashed by hand, this rustic dip retains a texture that is both creamy and chunky, making it uber-satisfying to eat. I could happily sit with a bowl of this, a few freshly toasted pittas and call it a day – a glass of Pinot wouldn't go amiss either, ahem. **Serves 2–4**

400g can butter beans
juice of 1 lemon
2 tablespoons extra virgin olive oil
1 tablespoon tahini
sea salt and freshly ground black pepper

FOR THE BASIL OIL:
30g fresh basil
juice of ½ lemon
2 tablespoons olive oil

1. Drain and rinse the butter beans, and then pop them from their skins. Put them in a shallow bowl and roughly mash with the back of a fork before adding half the lemon juice and a little salt and pepper. Mash further until the mixture starts to become creamy, then add the olive oil, tahini, remaining lemon juice and a touch more seasoning. Mix thoroughly until it becomes creamy and scoop-able, with a few small chunks still remaining.
2. Place all the basil oil ingredients in a food processor or mini blender and blend until it emulsifies – much like a dressing.
3. Spoon the dip into a serving bowl. Make waves in the dip using the back of a fork before drizzling over a tablespoon or so of the basil oil. Serve with crudités or toasted pitta, or use as a spread in sandwiches.

SMASHED CHICKPEA SANDWICH FILLER

Sandwiches are my weakness. I really can't think of a better lunch than a mega hunk of carb with a whole heap of filling spilling out from the inside... Because of this, I try to keep some sort of sandwich filler in the fridge at all times, so all that's required is for me to 'butter' some bread (or bagels – bagels work too!), lavish it with some smashed chickpea love and my lunchtime cravings are deftly (and deliciously) quashed. **Serves 2–4**

400g can chickpeas, drained, rinsed and preferably skins
   removed (see page 50)
juice of ½ lemon
½ small red onion, finely chopped
⅓ celery stick, finely chopped
¼ red pepper, deseeded and finely chopped
1 large sun-dried tomato, finely chopped
1 teaspoon Dijon mustard
1 tablespoon chopped dill
sea salt and freshly ground black pepper

1. Put the chickpeas in a large bowl and roughly mash using the back of a fork – it should have a coarse, nubbly texture. Spritz over a little lemon juice and season.
2. Add the red onion, celery, pepper and sun-dried tomato to the bowl. Stir to combine before adding the remaining lemon juice and mustard. Season to taste before finally forking through the chopped dill.
3. Use as a sandwich filler, toast topper or as an accompaniment to salads.

TIP: I like to toast a wholewheat bagel, spread it with a little vegan margarine, smother it in my smashed chickpea sandwich filler, add a few balsamic-dressed leaves and some sliced cucumber. Best. Combo. Ever.

Open sandwiches are my new obsession. I often keep a batch or two of spreads in the fridge so that all I have to do when the mood strikes is to reach for a slice of rye or pumpernickel and get topping. You could obviously play around with any variety of combinations yourself but here are three of my most relied-upon options that frequently make my lunches feel that little bit more special.

SCANDINAVIAN-STYLE OPEN SANDWICHES

BEETROOT *with a* MINTED PEA PURÉE

Serves 1–2

100g defrosted peas
1 heaped teaspoon dried mint
1 heaped tablespoon coconut cream
1 tablespoon extra virgin olive oil
rye or pumpernickel bread, to serve
1 small pre-cooked vacuum-packed
  beetroot (not in vinegar), sliced
1 tablespoon crushed mixed seeds,
  such as pumpkin, sesame and
  sunflower
sea salt and freshly ground
  black pepper

1. Put the peas, mint, coconut cream and some seasoning in a food processor or mini blender. Drizzle in the olive oil while it is blending until a coarse paste is formed. Check for seasoning and refrigerate until needed.
2. To assemble your sandwich, lightly toast the rye or pumpernickel bread. Generously spread with the pea purée and layer on the sliced beetroot. Season with a little salt, ground black pepper, a drizzle of extra virgin olive oil and a smattering of seeds.

TOMATO, EASY CASHEW CHEESE *and* RED ONION

Serves 1–2

rye or sunflower seed bread, to serve
1 tomato, sliced
½ small red onion, finely sliced
1 teaspoon capers

FOR THE EASY CASHEW CHEESE SPREAD:
100g soaked cashews (see page 120)
juice of ½ lemon
1 garlic clove, crushed
1 teaspoon cider vinegar
¼ teaspoon Dijon mustard
sea salt and freshly ground
  black pepper
1 tablespoon chopped fresh chives
  (optional)

1. Put the soaked cashews in a food processor with the lemon juice, grated garlic, cider vinegar, Dijon and some seasoning. Blend until it begins to form a thick, coarse, paste. It may take up to 10 minutes to achieve the desired consistency – add a tablespoon or so of water if necessary. It will go through several stages so be patient, scraping down the sides and underneath the blade with a spatula as and when necessary. Stir through the chives, check for seasoning and refrigerate until needed.
2. To assemble your sandwich, spread 2 tablespoons of the cashew cheese onto a large slice of rye or sunflower seed bread. Season the tomato and layer on top along with some red onion and a sprinkling of capers.

QUICK PICKLED CUCUMBER *and* CANNELLINI BEAN SANDWICH

GLUTEN FREE

Serves 1–2

¼ cucumber, peeled and sliced into
  thin rounds
1 tablespoon cider vinegar
1 teaspoon agave nectar
10g fresh dill, finely chopped
pumperknickel bread, to serve
salad cress, to serve

FOR THE CANNELLINI BEAN AND BEETROOT SPREAD:
1 rosemary sprig
1 garlic clove
juice of 1 lemon
3 tablespoons extra virgin olive oil
1 teaspoon salt
360g can cannellini beans, drained
  and rinsed
1 small pre-cooked vacuum-packed
  beetroot (not in vinegar)

1. Put the rosemary, garlic, lemon juice, olive oil and salt in a pestle and mortar and muddle until it renders a fragrant, pourable oil. Strain through a small tea strainer.
2. Put the cannellini beans and beetroot in a food processor or blender and gradually add the strained oil. Season generously and blitz into a thick, spreadable purée.
3. Put the cucumber in a shallow bowl. Lightly whisk the vinegar and agave together, pour over the cucumber and set aside for several minutes, then stir in the dill.
4. To assemble, generously spread some pumpernickel bread with the cannellini bean spread, top with the pickled cucumber and finish with some salad cress.

TOFU RICOTTA TOAST

This tofu ricotta makes a terrific toast topper, especially when paired with sliced nectarine – it really is a match made in heaven. You could, of course, add your own twist by throwing in some dried herbs or even a splash of balsamic vinegar. Think of it as a base, which you can dress up any way you fancy. **Serves 2–4**

200g firm tofu
juice of ½ lemon
1 tablespoon extra virgin olive oil
sea salt and freshly ground black
  pepper

TO SERVE:
1 nectarine, sliced
small handful of pistachios, crushed
fresh bread
agave nectar, to drizzle

1. Drain and press the tofu following the instructions on page 55.
2. Crumble the tofu directly onto a clean chopping board and season generously. Drizzle over the lemon juice and oil and mash with the back of a fork until it resembles ricotta.
3. Check for seasoning (it may need a little more salt) and mash again until there are no large lumps left. Refrigerate until needed – it will keep for up to a week in the fridge.
4. Toast some fresh bread and spread generously with the tofu ricotta. Top with the sliced nectarine, crushed pistachios and a drizzle of agave.

ULTIMATE GRIDDLED SWEET POTATO SANDWICH

Time to make our sandwich dreams come true, here with a show-stopping tower of all my favourite ingredients... namely bread, avocado, tomato, spinach and sweet potato. To top it all off, I've added a mouthwatering coriander cream that is sure to satisfy. **Serves 2**

1 small sweet potato, cut into
  1cm rounds
olive oil, for brushing
4 slices of sourdough, lightly
  toasted
1 avocado, peeled and stoned
lemon juice – just a drizzle
1 large tomato, thickly sliced
handful of spinach leaves
sea salt and freshly ground black
  pepper

FOR THE CORIANDER CREAM:
100g blanched soaked almonds
  (see page 120)
200ml water
1 teaspoon cider vinegar
1 teaspoon Dijon mustard
30g fresh coriander

1. First, make the coriander cream. Drain the soaked nuts and transfer to a high-speed blender. Add the water and blend until smooth. Season, add the cider vinegar, Dijon and coriander and blend until completely incorporated. Check for seasoning and refrigerate until needed.
2. Heat a non-stick griddle pan. Brush the sweet potato rounds with oil and griddle them for

8–10 minutes on each side until marked on both sides – they should pierce easily when prodded with a knife but still retain their form and texture. Set aside until needed.
3. Lay out the toasted sourdough on a board or plate. Divide one half of the avocado between two of the slices and mash. Season and squeeze over a touch of lemon juice. On the other slices, spread a thin layer of the coriander cream.
4. Season the tomato slices and layer them on top of the avocado, followed by the spinach, then the sweet potato. Spoon over the cream and add the remaining avocado – spooned, smashed or sliced. Press the other toasted sourdough slices firmly on top and serve.

BROCCOLI *and* QUINOA BITES

Quinoa is an absolute nutritional powerhouse but, being vegan, I love it mainly for its protein properties and also, more importantly, its quirky little form. I don't know any other food that can claim to be crunchy and fluffy in equal measures but quinoa manages to pull it off. You can make these patties as large or as little as you like but I'm all about the bite-size variety, which I usually dip into spicy vegan mayo or serve as a topping to my mega leafy salads. They hold together so well though, you could easily pop them between a bun for an awesome, protein-filled burger – it's entirely up to you! **Serves 4–6**

1 small head of broccoli

100g quinoa

2 garlic cloves, crushed

juice of ½ lemon

1 tablespoon olive oil, plus extra for frying

1 tablespoon nutritional yeast (optional), see page 10

2 heaped tablespoons plain flour

sea salt and freshly ground black pepper

1. Bring a large saucepan of water to the boil. Roughly chop the broccoli including some of the stalk, add to the pan and gently simmer until very soft. Drain and set aside to cool slightly.

2. Cover the quinoa with 1 cup of water in a saucepan, bring to the boil, cover, then reduce to a simmer until all the water has been fully absorbed.

3. Finely chop the cooked broccoli until there are no large pieces left. Combine the broccoli with the cooked quinoa, garlic, lemon juice, oil and some seasoning. Once fully combined, sprinkle over the nutritional yeast, if using, and flour, and mix until the mixture begins to come together and can be easily formed into small patties.

4. Heat a tablespoon or so of oil in a heavy-based non-stick frying pan. Ensure the oil is not too hot or your patties may disintegrate; a medium heat is best. Take a heaped tablespoon of the mixture, roll into a rough ball, then shape into a patty, flattening slightly between your palms. Gently fry each patty for 5–7 minutes on each side until golden on both sides. Keep warm in a low oven until all the mixture is used.

5. Serve with a side of spicy mayo and a dressed baby leaf salad.

CHILLED CUCUMBER SOUP *with a* TAHINI COCONUT DRIZZLE

Even if you're not a cucumber fan; even if you're reluctant to eat cold soup, I implore you to try this anyway. The coconut tahini drizzle is crucial in balancing out the flavours and giving it that necessary oomph, rendering this simple summer starter a perfect addition to those lazy, hazy meals that linger in the mind – and hopefully on the taste buds. Don't believe me? I dare you to try it for yourself. **Serves 2–3**

⅓ cucumber, peeled and deseeded
½ avocado, peeled and stoned
1 spring onion
1 tablespoon coconut cream
juice of ½ lime
150–200ml water
sea salt and freshly ground black pepper

FOR THE TAHINI COCONUT DRIZZLE:
2 tablespoons tahini
2 tablespoons coconut cream
1 small garlic clove, finely minced
juice of 1 lime
2–3 tablespoons water
1 heaped tablespoon freshly chopped coriander, plus extra to garnish

1. First, make the tahini coconut drizzle. Whisk all the ingredients, except the coriander, together until smooth. Stir through the chopped coriander and chill until needed.
2. Put all the soup ingredients in a food processor or blender, using 150ml of the water initially, and blend until smooth. Taste for seasoning and also texture – if it's too thick to be strained, it may require a touch more water. It should be the consistency of gazpacho.
3. Once blended, strain through a fine-mesh sieve or, ideally, a nut milk bag and chill for at least 1 hour.
4. Once the soup has sufficiently chilled, serve in small shallow bowls, adorned with sliced or chopped avocado, a swirl of the tahini coconut drizzle and a final smattering of fresh coriander.

THAI-INSPIRED SPIRALISED SALAD

If you haven't jumped aboard the spiralised bandwagon already, this Thai-inspired salad is the perfect introduction. It might seem like a bit of an investment (and truthfully it took me a while to purchase one myself) but as soon as you sample those tasty swirls there really is no going back. However, should you not be in the market for another kitchen gadget, a good back-up plan is to shred the vegetables into ribbons using a peeler and proceed as normal. Your crunchy, tangy, tamarind future awaits. **Serves 2**

1 cucumber, spiralised (or peeled into ribbons with a vegetable peeler)
2 courgettes, spiralised (or peeled into ribbons with a vegetable peeler)
70g cashews
sesame oil, to drizzle
½ mango, peeled and diced
1 large red chilli, deseeded and finely sliced
30g fresh coriander, chopped, plus extra to serve

FOR THE TAMARIND DRESSING:
1 tablespoon tamarind paste
1 tablespoon tamari or soy sauce (please note that if you use soy sauce, the recipe will not be gluten-free)
1 tablespoon maple syrup
juice of 1 lime

1. Preheat the oven to 200°C/gas mark 6. Put the cucumber and courgette spirals in a large bowl. Place the dressing ingredients in a bowl and whisk until they fully amalgamate.
2. Pour half the dressing over the spiralised vegetables and thoroughly mix. Set aside for about 10–15 minutes to allow the vegetables to fully marinate.
3. Toss the cashews in the remaining dressing and drizzle over a smidge of sesame oil to avoid sticking. Tip into a baking tray and roast for about 15 minutes until toasted, making sure to shake the baking dish from time to time. Remove from oven and leave to cool completely.
4. Add the mango and chilli to the spiralised vegetables and toss to combine along with the chopped coriander and some of the roasted cashews, reserving a few for garnish.
5. Transfer the salad to a serving dish. Garnish with the remaining cashews and a final smattering of coriander.

GLUTEN FREE

QUICK PICKLED RADISH

I'm a bit of a sucker for a pickle but I possess very little patience when it comes to making them. Step in this super-easy, quick pickled radish that can be made in minutes and ready to use almost instantly. I often use these wafer-thin lovelies to garnish open sandwiches but they also work really well in salads or as a topping for dips. Be warned though, the pickling vinegar is so pungent it will waft through your kitchen in all its sweetly spiced glory for quite some time... something I'm happy to suffer through for an antioxidant-boosting preserve that can be made in a snap. **Serves 2–4**

120ml red wine vinegar
120ml water
60ml agave nectar
1 heaped teapoon salt
1 tablespoon black peppercorns
1 star anise
100g radishes

1. Place all the ingredients, except the radishes, in a saucepan and simmer gently for 20 minutes until it reduces.
2. Finely slice the radishes (a mandolin is a good device to use in this instance) and place them in a clean 240g jar.
3. Pour the pickling vinegar into the jar, including the star anise and peppercorns, seal and set aside to cool. It is ready to use once the contents are completely cool, and will keep for about a fortnight.

TIPS: The pickling vinegar works really well with red cabbage and red onion too. To sterilise your jar before use, wash well in soapy water, rinse with freshly boiled water and then dry in a medium oven for a few minutes.

EASY MEALS

TORTILLA SOUP
MUSHROOM *and* TARRAGON SOUP
  with a ROCKET *and* WALNUT GREMOLATA
ROASTED TOMATO SOUP
  with ROSEMARY-ROASTED SALAD POTATOES
GREEN LENTIL *and* SPINACH CURRY
SMOKY ORZO JAMBALAYA
SWEETCORN-STUFFED POTATO SKINS
CRUNCHY BROCCOLI and CARROT SALAD
  with a GINGER GARLIC DRESSING
MISO-MARINATED MUSHROOMS
RED CABBAGE COLESLAW
QUINOA TABBOULEH *with* HARISSA DRESSING
CRUNCHY CAULIFLOWER COUSCOUS
  with ROASTED FIGS
VIETNAMESE NOODLE BOWL
BULGAR WHEAT BOWL with ROASTED VEGGIES
SUPER-EASY, SUPER-GREEN,
  SUNDAY NIGHT SPAGHETTI
BUTTON MUSHROOM and CHICKPEA PIES
WALNUT MEAT TACOS
BLACK BEAN TAQUITOS
  with an ENCHILADA SAUCE

TORTILLA SOUP

This is a warming, filling weeknight meal that caters to my lingering Mexican obsession. Not too spicy, and with a breadth of flavour, I often opt for something like this to see me through a tough week... in fact, I frequently make it in advance and reheat as and when needed. The crispy tortilla strips are what it's all about though (hence the name!) and really add to the already magnificent array of textures in the bowl. I'd be very surprised if this doesn't quickly become a firm favourite in your kitchen, too. **Serves 4**

olive oil, for frying, plus 1 tablespoon for the tortilla
1 red onion, finely chopped
½ fennel bulb, finely chopped
1 celery stick, finely chopped
3 garlic cloves, sliced
1 red pepper, deseeded and finely chopped
1 small courgette, finely chopped
1 red chilli, deseeded and sliced
1 heaped teaspoon smoked paprika
½ teaspoon ground cumin
pinch of cayenne pepper
400g can plum tomatoes
150g sweetcorn kernels
200g canned kidney beans, drained and rinsed
1 tablespoon tomato purée
1 large flour tortilla
1 ripe avocado, peeled, stoned and diced
fresh coriander leaves and lime juice, to serve
sea salt and freshly ground black pepper

1. Heat a little oil in a large saucepan. Add the red onion, fennel and celery to the pan. Season, cover and sweat gently until they begin to soften before adding the garlic. Sauté for a further 5 minutes until fragrant.

2. Add the red pepper, courgette and chilli. Season, cover and sweat gently until soft.

3. Sprinkle in the spices, season, cover and let them infuse for a few minutes before tipping in the plum tomatoes. Simmer for about 5 minutes to soften before breaking up the tomatoes with the back of a spoon. Season generously and add 1.5 litres water. Add the sweetcorn, kidney beans and tomato purée and bring to a very gentle simmer for about 20 minutes – be sure not to let the soup boil.

4. While the soup is warming, preheat the oven to 200°C/gas mark 6. Cut the tortilla into small strips, toss in 1 tablespoon oil, lay out on a baking tray and bake for 10–12 minutes until golden, turning once.

5. Divide the soup between four bowls and adorn each with the crunchy tortilla strips, some diced avocado, a smattering of coriander and some fresh lime juice.

MUSHROOM *and* TARRAGON SOUP *with a* ROCKET *and* WALNUT GREMOLATA

GLUTEN FREE

Tarragon is frequently the forgotten herb, and while I can't claim to use it in abundance myself, I like to utilise a smattering of its 'aniseedy' overtones in a variety of my favourite dishes – and, yes, mushroom soup happens to be one of them. This particular dish is rich, earthy and deeply flavourful, and even though I suggest dividing it between two bowls, I could easily consume the lot myself. The gremolata adds some necessary texture to what can only be described, in my own inimitable over-the-top way, as my homegrown Irish girl's answer to the 'nectar of the Gods' – told you I loved this soup! **Serves 2–3**

1–2 tablespoons olive oil
1 red onion, finely chopped
3 garlic cloves, crushed
250g chestnut mushrooms, roughly chopped
15g tarragon, roughly chopped
juice of ½ lemon
1 vegetable stock cube
splash of soya cream, plus extra to serve
sea salt and freshly ground black pepper

FOR THE GREMOLATA:
handful of rocket
1 tablespoon walnuts
1 tablespoon sunflower seeds
lemon juice
1 tablespoon extra virgin olive oil

1. Heat a tablespoon or so of olive oil in a heavy-based saucepan. Add the red onion to the pan, season and gently cook until translucent.

2. Add the garlic to the pan and sauté for several minutes before adding the mushrooms to the pan. Season and sauté until they begin to soften.

3. Add the tarragon to the pan along with the lemon juice and a touch of black pepper. Cook gently for a few minutes to let the flavours infuse. Cover with 1 litre water, add the stock cube and gently simmer for 10–15 minutes.

4. Transfer to a food processor or blender and blitz until completely smooth. Return to the pan, add a splash of soya cream and gently heat through.

5. While the soup is on the hob you can make the gremolata by using a knife to mince the rocket, walnuts and sunflower seeds on a chopping board. Season, squeeze over a little lemon juice and extra virgin olive oil and continue to mince until it forms a coarse, nutty rubble. Set aside until needed.

6. Divide the soup between two warmed bowls, drizzle over some soya cream and adorn with the gremolata.

ROASTED TOMATO SOUP *with* ROSEMARY-ROASTED SALAD POTATOES

Tomato soup conjures up so many memories for me – as I'm sure it does for many. These days, though, I'm more in the market for something a little healthier than the canned tomato soup of our youth... and, of course, something homemade. This roasted tomato recipe could not be simpler – it's just a case of putting it all in a dish and letting the oven do the hard work. Same goes for the spuds. So now instead of reaching for that familiar can of comfort, I opt for the roasted route instead. **Serves 2**

4 large tomatoes, halved
1 red onion, roughly chopped
3 garlic cloves, peeled
3 rosemary sprigs
1 tablespoon balsamic vinegar
2 tablespoons olive oil
1 tablespoon maple syrup
sea salt and freshly ground
   black pepper

FOR THE POTATOES:
400g salad potatoes, halved
2 rosemary sprigs, leaves finely
   chopped
1–2 tablespoons olive oil

1. Preheat the oven to 200°C/gas mark 6.
2. Put the tomatoes and red onion in a large baking dish. Scatter over the garlic and rosemary sprigs, and drizzle over the balsamic, olive oil and maple syrup. Season generously and roast for about 1 hour until the tomatoes are thoroughly cooked and bubbling.
3. Meanwhile, prepare the potatoes. Put the potatoes in a small baking dish and scatter over the rosemary. Season and coat in a tablespoon or so of oil. Roast for about 45 minutes until crispy and golden.
4. Carefully transfer the roasted tomatoes to a food processor or blender, then blend until smooth. Pour into a saucepan and add 500ml water (or a little more for a thinner soup), check for seasoning and gently warm over a low heat.
5. Divide the soup between two bowls and serve the roasted spuds in the centre.

GREEN LENTIL *and* SPINACH CURRY

I am by no means a curry expert. In fact, this recipe is a hotchpotch of various cuisines thrown together in one harmonious pot. Is it Indian? Nepalese? Who knows! What I am sure of is that it satiates those all too familiar take-away cravings and even though it takes what feels like an age on the hob, the result is absolutely worth the wait. Not too spicy with a rounded flavour thanks to the coconut milk, and small but crucial palm sugar addition... if you can't find palm sugar in your local supermarket, just use plain old brown sugar. I know sugar is currently on the nutritional death list but I find a smattering here and there can really make a huge difference to a sauce. **Serves 2–4**

1 tablespoon coconut oil
1 onion, chopped
1 carrot, chopped
1 garlic clove
thumb-size piece of fresh ginger
1 red chilli
125g dried green lentils
400ml can coconut milk
½ gluten-free vegetable stock cube
1 tablespoon tomato purée
150g spinach
30g fresh coriander, roughly chopped
sea salt and freshly ground black pepper
brown rice, to serve

FOR THE CUCUMBER AND COCONUT DRESSING:
¼ small cucumber
2 tablespoons coconut cream
juice of ½ lime
1 spring onion, finely chopped
pinch of salt

FOR THE CURRY POWDER:
3 cardamom pods
½ teaspoon garam masala
½ teaspoon palm sugar or other vegan sweetener
a few black peppercorns
pinch of cayenne pepper

1. First make the dressing. Deseed and finely grate the cucumber, squeezing out any excess juice. Whisk together with the other dressing ingredients, but be sure not to over-season. Refrigerate until needed.

2. Next, grind the curry powder ingredients together in a pestle and mortar to a fine powder.
3. Heat the oil in a large heavy-based frying pan. Add the onion and carrot to the pan, season and sweat for several minutes until they begin to soften.
4. Using a knife, mince the garlic, ginger and chilli together on a clean chopping board and add them to the pan. Cover and sweat until fragrant before tossing in the dried lentils. Stir to coat and let the lentils absorb any flavours in the pan before sprinkling over the prepared curry powder. Cover and sweat for several minutes until the spices become nicely toasted and the flavours have penetrated the veg and lentils.
5. Add the coconut milk, stock cube and 150ml water, cover and simmer gently over a medium heat for about 1 hour until the lentils cook through.
6. Stir through the tomato purée and boil the sauce, uncovered, for about 10 minutes to reduce before adding the spinach to the pan. Cover and let the spinach leaves wilt into the sauce.
7. Add almost all of the coriander to the pan, reserving a little for a garnish. Once the sauce has sufficiently reduced and the spinach leaves have wilted, serve over a bed of brown rice with a spoonful of the cucumber and coconut dressing.

SMOKY ORZO JAMBALAYA

This is such a speedy week-night recipe that requires very little prep or thought. I just love using orzo in place of rice – in fact, cooking it this way is my preferred method. I've dubbed it 'jambalaya' because it reminds me of a recipe I discovered in the States... and also because I'm a bit of a (read massive) Carpenters fan. It's smoky, sweet and super filling – credentials crucial for a midweek meal in my opinion.

Serves 2–3

1 tablespoon olive oil
1 onion, finely chopped
3 garlic cloves, crushed
1 red chilli, deseeded and finely chopped
1 large red pepper, deseeded and roughly chopped
handful of cherry tomatoes, halved
1 heaped teaspoon smoked paprika
200g orzo
1 litre vegetable stock
50g frozen peas
50g sweetcorn kernels, frozen or canned
sea salt and freshly ground black pepper

TO SERVE:
30g fresh flat-leaf parsley, torn
extra virgin olive oil, for drizzling
chilli flakes, for sprinkling

1. Heat the oil in a large frying pan. Add the onion, season and sauté until translucent. Add the garlic and chilli and lightly sauté over a medium heat for several minutes until fragrant.
2. Add the red pepper to the pan along with the cherry tomatoes. Season generously, add the smoked paprika and sauté until the pepper begins to soften.
3. Stir through the orzo and let it absorb the flavours before pouring over the vegetable stock. Simmer gently until all the liquid has been absorbed, stirring frequently to prevent sticking. Stir through the peas and sweetcorn and heat through, adding a little more water if necessary to prevent the orzo from catching on the base of the pan.
4. Season and serve with more parsley, a generous drizzle of extra virgin oil and a smattering of chilli flakes and sea salt.

SWEETCORN-STUFFED POTATO SKINS

The humble baked potato is mightily under-appreciated in my opinion, and the tendency to microwave them must be partly to blame. I feel it's my duty then to bring back the jacket in all its crispy exterior, fluffy interior glory. Yes, it's a simple dish, but one that can all too often go wrong – I have zero tolerance for soggy potato skins. The trick lies in pricking the skin all over, rubbing it with oil and salt and placing it directly onto the oven shelf. That's correct, no baking trays or dishes, just plonk those bad boys on the bare bars and you'll find yourself with one perfect baked potato. As I'm also partial to a stuffed spud, I've gone one step further and this is the result – just a tad more special. By all means use sweet potatoes if you prefer – same rules apply.

Serves 2–4

2 large baking potatoes
olive oil, for rubbing and frying
2 tablespoons soya cream
1 tablespoon diced red pepper
1 tablespoon diced yellow pepper
1 corn on the cob
¼ teaspoon smoked paprika
pinch of cayenne pepper
1 spring onion, sliced
1 teaspoon Dijon mustard
nutritional yeast (see page 10), for sprinkling (optional, but please note that, if you use it, this dish will not be gluten-free)
sea salt and freshly ground black pepper

TO SERVE:
1 heaped tablespoon chopped chives
4 tablespoons Soured Cashew Cream (page 121)

1. Preheat the oven to 200°C/gas mark 6. Prick the potatoes all over with a fork, rub them in olive oil and salt and place directly onto the oven shelf. Bake for about 1 hour until crispy on the outside.

2. Let the potatoes cool for a few minutes before halving and scooping out the soft insides into a large bowl. Season, add the cream and roughly mash with the back of a fork.

3. Heat a small amount of oil in a frying pan and add the peppers. Season and fry quickly over a high heat until they begin to soften and colour.

4. Heat a griddle pan over a high heat. Rub the corn on the cob with a little oil and griddle until slightly charred. Using a sharp knife, slice off the kernels and add to the pan with the peppers. Season with smoked paprika and cayenne and stir fry for a minute or two before adding the spring onion and stir frying until slightly softened.

5. Add the sweetcorn mix to the mashed potatoes along with the Dijon mustard. Season generously and stir to combine.

6. Spoon the mixture back into the skins, sprinkle over a little nutritional yeast (if using), place on a baking tray and bake for 30 minutes until golden brown.

7. Stir the chopped chives through the Cashew Soured Cream, adding a splash of Plant Milk (see page 28) to thin it out if necessary. Dollop a generous amount over the potato skins before serving.

GLUTEN FREE

CRUNCHY BROCCOLI *and* CARROT SALAD *with a* GINGER GARLIC DRESSING

Simplicity is at the core of my kitchen, and indeed, eating. I may give some thought to nutrients and whatnot but really I go on instinct... and, more importantly, taste. This salad is one such dish that brings me immense pleasure in the flavour department but also happens to be packed full of goodness too. In fact, I made this very dish for my father when he was recovering from surgery, and I'm positive it helped his body heal – ginger is terrific for nausea and garlic has a bounty of medicinal properties too. Putting all that to one side however, I think you'll be equally enamoured with its superb crunch, all brought to life by what can only be described as a winning salad dressing – just make sure you don't eat it before a date. **Serves 2**

½ head of broccoli, cut into small florets, stalks removed

2 carrots, grated

1 spring onion, finely sliced

30g fresh coriander leaves

2 tablespoons toasted flaked almonds (see Note, page 86)

FOR THE DRESSING

2 garlic cloves

thumb-size piece of fresh ginger, peeled

juice of ½ lemon

½ tablespoon agave nectar or other vegan sweetener

½ tablespoon cider vinegar

2 tablespoons olive oil

1. Mix the broccoli, carrot and spring onion together in a medium bowl.

2. To make the dressing, pound the garlic and ginger to a paste in a pestle and mortar. Add the remaining dressing ingredients and whisk vigorously until it emulsifies.

3. Pour half the dressing over the vegetables and mix thoroughly before adding most of the coriander, then the remaining dressing. Toss to combine, then stir through most of the flaked almonds.

4. Serve in a shallow dish and garnish with the remaining coriander and almonds.

EASY MEALS

81

MISO-MARINATED MUSHROOMS

Miso is such a uniquely powerful paste, I consider it a godsend to my vegan pantry, coming in especially handy when I need to inject some serious flavour. I use it in a multitude of dishes (not least as a robust base to soups) but I particularly adore it in marinades – specifically ones that benefit from being barbecued. Portobello mushrooms might seem like a tired choice for long-term vegans (can I get a 'yawn'!) but before you write them off completely, may I urge you to slather on this rich marinade and give them yet another whirl? If you really can't face another mushroom, however, this marinade is also sensational with roasted aubergines... simply halve and score an aubergine, then slather with the sauce before covering with foil and roasting for around 30 minutes or until soft. It's also great on tofu and even as a coating on roughly chopped roasted potatoes. **Serves 4**

4 portobello mushrooms

FOR THE MARINADE:
1 heaped tablespoon miso
1 teaspoon tamari sauce (you can also use soy sauce, but please note this is not gluten-free)
1 teaspoon sesame oil
1 tablespoon agave nectar
1 tablespoon olive oil
juice of 1 lime

TIP: These are great for the barbecue – simply put them on the hot grill for 30 minutes, turning once, and brush over the marinade until cooked.

1. Preheat the oven to 200°C/gas mark 6. Gently clean the mushrooms using kitchen paper or a clean cloth – do not remove the stalks.
2. Whisk the marinade ingredients together in a small bowl until smooth and glossy. Generously brush the marinade over the mushrooms, then set aside to absorb for at least 30 minutes. Reserve a little marinade for basting during cooking.
3. Place the mushrooms on a baking sheet and bake for 40 minutes, basting with the remaining marinade halfway through.
4. Serve the mushrooms in a bun, wrap or sliced alongside some creamy mash – my preferred choice.

RED CABBAGE COLESLAW

Coleslaw is high on my summer barbecue menu list. No gathering is complete without a large bowl of it alongside some fabulously marinated vegetables on the grill. Full of texture and tang, it's a world away from the mayo-clad coleslaw you probably remember as a child. The zingy Dijon mustard dressing brings the crunchy cabbage to life without masking any flavours, but be sure to slice everything as finely as possible to enjoy it at its best. If you don't have great knife skills, a mandolin is the perfect kitchen utensil for the job – just be careful of those precious digits. **Serves 4–6**

½ small red cabbage, finely sliced or shredded

1 large carrot, grated

½ red onion, finely sliced

handful of sugar snap peas, sliced diagonally

4 radishes, finely sliced (or 2 heaped tablespoons Quick Pickled Radish, see page 68)

1 heaped tablespoon pumpkin seeds

30g fresh coriander, roughly chopped

FOR THE SIMPLE DIJON DRESSING:

1 tablespoon Dijon mustard

1 tablespoon red wine vinegar

1 tablespoon agave nectar

2 tablespoons extra virgin olive oil

juice of ½ lemon

sea salt and freshly ground black pepper

1. Gently toss the cabbage and carrot together in a large salad bowl and add the red onion.

2. Add the sugar snap peas and radishes and mix thoroughly to combine the ingredients – this is best done using clean hands.

3. Whisk the dressing ingredients together in a separate bowl until they emulsify before pouring over the vegetables and stirring to combine.

4. Add the pumpkin seeds and coriander to the bowl and give it a final stir before serving.

QUINOA TABBOULEH *with* HARISSA DRESSING

As much as I love traditional tabbouleh, this quinoa version is always a welcome change. Using sun-dried tomatoes instead of fresh and with perhaps a teensy bit less parsley than is the norm... but enough to qualify it as an actual 'tabbouleh' salad of sorts. I serve it as a side but it's also great in wraps – simply stuff, roll and eat. **Serves 2–4**

250g quinoa
juice of ½ lemon
1 spring onion, finely chopped
1 celery stick, finely chopped
6 sun-dried tomatoes, chopped
20g fresh mint, finely chopped
150g fresh flat-leaf parsley, finely chopped
30g pumpkin seeds
50g pine nuts, toasted
sea salt and freshly ground black pepper

FOR THE HARISSA DRESSING:
1 heaped teaspoon harissa paste
juice of ½ lemon
1 teaspoon red wine vinegar
1 tablespoon olive oil
1 teaspoon agave nectar

1. Rinse the quinoa thoroughly, then place in a saucepan. Cover with water (I use one part quinoa to two parts water), clamp on a lid and simmer until all the liquid has been absorbed. Set aside to cool, then fluff with a fork.
2. Once cool, put the quinoa in a bowl, squeeze over the lemon juice and generously season. Stir to combine.
3. Add the spring onion, celery and sun-dried tomatoes to the quinoa and stir to combine.
4. Put all the dressing ingredients in a bowl along with some seasoning and whisk thoroughly. Pour over the quinoa and stir to combine.
5. Add the herbs, pumpkin seeds and pine nuts to the bowl. Check for seasoning, give a final, thorough stir and serve at room temperature.

EASY MEALS

CRUNCHY CAULIFLOWER COUSCOUS *with* ROASTED FIGS

While most of us associate cauliflower with cheese, this dish couldn't be further from those school-dinner days with a vibrant array of flavours that are less 'Sunday roast' and more 'Middle Eastern promise'. Packed full of crunch, texture and that elusive 'umami' – thanks to some delicate spice additions, sweet roasted figs and a delightfully easy hummus dressing – this simple side is bound to become your new favourite way to serve a comfortingly familiar ingredient. For that carb-like experience without the calories or typical bloated aftermath (we've all been there) make this grain-free couscous your go-to dinnertime dish. Serves 2

NOTE: To toast almond flakes, heat a frying pan over a medium heat, add the almonds and toast for about 10 minutes. Stir frequently and be sure to keep an eye on them, as they turn from toasted to burnt in a matter of seconds. Set aside until needed.

1 small cauliflower, broken into florets
1 heaped teaspoon coconut oil
2 shallots, finely diced
1 large carrot, finely diced
2 garlic cloves, grated
1cm piece of fresh ginger, grated
1 heaped teaspoon Quick Preserved Lemons (page 58)
handful of raisins
handful of toasted flaked almonds
sea salt and freshly ground black pepper

FOR THE RAS EL HANOUT:
1 heaped teaspoon ground cumin
1 teaspoon ground coriander
1 teaspoon turmeric
½ teaspoon ground ginger
½ teaspoon allspice
½ teaspoon paprika
¼ teaspoon cinnamon
¼ teaspoon freshly grated nutmeg

FOR THE ROASTED FIGS:
2 ripe figs
1 teaspoon coconut oil
drizzle of agave nectar and pomegranate molasses

FOR THE COURGETTE DRESSING:
4 heaped tablespoons Creamy Courgette Dip (page 58)
juice of ½ lemon

1. Preheat the oven to 180°C/gas mark 4.

2. Prepare the roasted figs. Run a knife through the figs so that they form quarters but be sure to leave them attached at the bottom. Grease a small ovenproof dish with the coconut oil. Place the figs in the dish, drizzle with agave and pomegranate molasses and sprinkle over some salt. Roast for 25–30 minutes or until they are soft and juicy.

3. Meanwhile, put the cauliflower in a food processor and pulse until it becomes like couscous.

4. Heat the coconut oil in a heavy-based frying pan. Add the shallots, carrot, garlic and ginger and fry over a medium heat until they begin to soften. Fry for 5 minutes before adding the cauliflower couscous.

5. Add the ras el hanout spices to the pan and stir-fry for about 10 minutes. Take off the heat and stir through the Quick Preserved Lemons and raisins. Check for seasoning and set aside to cool for a few minutes before adding the flaked almonds, reserving a few for serving.

6. Whisk the Courgette Dip with the lemon juice and a little black pepper in a bowl to form a smooth sauce.

7. Serve the couscous in a wide bowl or plate and top with the roasted figs. Sprinkle over a few flaked almonds and garnish with the dressing.

VIETNAMESE NOODLE BOWL

More a nod to the almighty 'Bun' bowl than an actual authentic replication but I adore it nonetheless. You could really add anything to the veg part but I'm seriously digging the spiralised sweet potato and teriyaki-roasted squash combo that is pretty much out of this world. I'm positively gaga about the toppings too – just remember to mix everything together before diving in, lest you end up with an underwhelming mouthful of rice noodle *sans* sauce. Talking of sauces, you could really use anything you fancy but I'm all about the depth of flavour this mega homemade peanut sauce brings to the bowl, rendering it a non-negotiable recipe addition. Oh, and p.s. this is a dish best served at room temp, so don't worry about the sauce and/or noodles remaining piping hot. Pressure. Off. **Serves 2**

½ butternut squash, peeled and diced
3 tablespoons soy sauce, plus extra to serve
2 tablespoons teriyaki sauce, plus extra to serve
1 tablespoon sesame oil
1 tablespoon rapeseed oil, plus extra for frying
1 garlic clove
thumb-size piece of fresh ginger
1 red chilli
1 sweet potato, spiralised
½ tablespoon tamari sauce
5 tablespoons freshly chopped coriander
45g rice noodles
50g canned sweetcorn kernels
3-4 radishes, finely sliced
1 spring onion, finely chopped
1 tablespoon sesame seeds
1 tablespoon crushed peanuts
pinch of chilli flakes
hot sauce (such as sriracha or sambal oelek), to serve

FOR THE PEANUT SAUCE:
2 tablespoons peanut butter
½ tablespoon soy sauce or tamari
½ tablespoon agave nectar or maple syrup
½ tablespoon teriyaki sauce
½ tablespoon sambal olek
½ tablespoon sesame oil
juice of ½ lime

1. Preheat the oven to 200°C/gas mark 6.
2. Put the squash in a baking dish and toss with the soy sauce, teriyaki and oils. Roast for about 40 minutes until soft and caramelised, shaking the dish from time to time for an even bake.
3. Meanwhile, heat some rapeseed oil in a pan. Mince the garlic, ginger and chilli together on a clean chopping board and add to the pan. Gently sweat until fragrant before adding the sweet potato. Drizzle over the tamari sauce. Add a splash or two of water and allow the sweet potato to cook for a few minutes until it just begins to soften. Toss in 4 tablespoons of the coriander and set aside.
4. Pour freshly boiled water over the rice noodles and leave them to steep for about 3–4 minutes before draining and rinsing, then set aside.
5. In a bowl, whisk together the peanut sauce ingredients with 2–3 tablespoons water until smooth.
6. Divide the noodles and sweet potato between two deep bowls and spoon the roasted squash over the noodles, preferably to one side. Garnish with the sweetcorn, radish, spring onion, sesame seeds, crushed peanuts, chilli flakes and remaining coriander, and pour over some peanut sauce. Pour over the hot sauce and mix thoroughly before eating.

BULGAR WHEAT BOWL *with* ROASTED VEGGIES

This is another super-simple dish I regularly turn to when I don't have much time to fuss in the kitchen. Besides giving the veggie pan a shake now and then, you can just let it do its thing in the oven and go about your business. I often serve this alongside my favourite baked falafels (see page 51) but if I'm in a real rush then I'll just chuck in some chickpeas at the end before drizzling over a simple tahini dressing to finish. Perfection in a bowl. **Serves 2–4**

1 red pepper, deseeded and roughly chopped
1 yellow pepper, deseeded and roughly chopped
1 white or red onion, roughly chopped
1 small aubergine, roughly chopped
1 tablespoon olive oil
1 teaspoon dried mixed herbs
100g bulgar wheat
1 lemon, halved
100g canned chickpeas (optional, if not serving with falafel)
small bunch (about 40g) fresh flat-leaf parsley, roughly chopped
small bunch (about 40g) fresh coriander, roughly chopped
1 tablespoon sunflower seeds
sea salt and freshly ground black pepper

1. Preheat the oven to 200°C/gas mark 6.
2. Put the vegetables in a shallow baking dish and toss with the oil, herbs and seasoning. Roast for about 1 hour until soft and slightly charred around the edges, shaking the pan from time to time.
3. Place the bulgar wheat in a bowl. Squeeze over half the lemon cover with about 100ml freshly boiled water. Cover and set aside until all the liquid has been absorbed. Fluff with a fork and squeeze in any remaining juice from the lemon half.
4. Transfer the bulgar wheat (and the chickpeas, if using) to the dish the vegetables were cooked in and thoroughly mix, allowing the wheat to absorb any residual juices. Squeeze over the remaining half lemon before finally stirring through the herbs and seeds.

SUPER-EASY, SUPER-GREEN, SUNDAY NIGHT SPAGHETTI

It doesn't happen too often but whenever the will to cook has really left me I often turn to dishes like this... bish, bash, bosh, in my belly. A short-cut to satisfaction it might be but rest assured I still want my nutritional fix with that little bit of added comfort too – and nothing spells comfort food like a warming bowl of spaghetti, am I right? The fact it can be made all in the one pot also saves on the washing-up, making it the perfect lazy Sunday supper option with oodles of flavour and no stress. **Serves 2–3**

200g wholewheat spaghetti
100g green beans
handful of fresh rocket
balsamic vinegar
extra virgin olive or flaxseed oil
sea salt and freshly ground black pepper

FOR THE PESTO:
30g fresh basil leaves
30g spinach
2 tablespoons mixed nuts (walnuts
   and pecans work best)
juice of ½ lemon
1 small garlic clove
3 tablespoons extra virgin olive oil
3 tablespoons flaxseed oil

1. Bring a large saucepan of salted water to the boil and add the spaghetti.
2. Place all the pesto ingredients in a food processor or mini blender and blend until smooth. Taste for seasoning and add a touch more salt and pepper if necessary.
3. Once the spaghetti has been boiling for about 5 minutes, add the green beans and cook for a further 4–5 minutes or until the pasta is al dente and the beans are cooked.
4. Retain a cup of the cooking liquid and drain the spaghetti. Return the spaghetti and beans to the pan, add the pesto and half the reserved cooking liquid and stir thoroughly to combine. Add more liquid if necessary.
5. Dress the rocket leaves in a little balsamic vinegar, oil and seasoning. Serve the spaghetti in warmed bowls and top each with a handful of dressed rocket leaves. Healthy comfort food ready to go!

BUTTON MUSHROOM *and* CHICKPEA PIES

I'm an unashamed ready-made pastry addict. It doesn't worry me a jot that it's considered a cheat's way out. And let's be totally honest, it's all about the filling anyway, right? The button mushroom and chickpea combo is hearty, meaty and filling with just enough background heat to keep it interesting. This is the perfect midweek dish. Serves 2

1 tablespoon olive oil
1 onion, roughly chopped
1 carrot, roughly chopped
1 celery, roughly chopped
1 garlic clove, finely sliced
220g button mushrooms
1 tablespoon red wine vinegar
1 tablespoon dried mixed herbs,
   such as herbes de Provence
generous pinch of chilli flakes
100g canned chickpeas, drained and rinsed
handful of sliced spinach leaves
1 vegetable stock cube
1 tablespoon plain flour
1 x large sheet ready-made puff pastry
1 tablespoon Plant Milk (see page 28)
sea salt and freshly ground black pepper

1. Preheat the oven to 200°C/gas mark 6.
2. Heat the olive oil in a large saucepan. Add the onion, carrot and celery. Season and sauté until they begin to soften.
3. Add the garlic to the pan and gently fry until fragrant before tumbling in the button mushrooms whole. Season, cover and leave them to sweat for several minutes before adding the red wine vinegar.
4. Once the vinegar has evaporated, add the chopped herbs and chilli flakes. Cover and sauté for 5 minutes until the mushrooms begin to exude their juices.

5. Add the chickpeas and spinach and season generously with black pepper. Stir and let the spinach wilt before covering with water and finally adding the stock cube. Simmer gently for about 10 minutes.
6. Add the flour and whisk immediately until it dissolves into the stock and the sauce begins to thicken. Simmer for a further 5 minutes before removing from the heat.
7. Unroll your sheet of puff pastry and cut four even strips from the end. Turn your pudding bowls upside down and cut around the outside using a sharp knife until you have a lid for each.
8. Use your fingers to dampen the rim of your bowls with a little plant milk and firmly press two strips of pastry around the edges – this will help the lid adhere to the bowl. Carefully divide the pie filling between each bowl and top with your pastry lid, crimping the edges with a fork. Make several small holes in the centre of each lid using a sharp knife (you could also brush the tops with a smidge more plant milk if you like) and bake for about 20 minutes or until the tops are golden. Serve immediately.

WALNUT MEAT TACOS

Even if the idea of raw food really doesn't float your boat, these walnut meat tacos are a great way of easing yourself into a wonderfully vibrant cuisine. Like any traditional taco, they are a harmonious layering of texture and flavour, and so satisfying you'll soon forget they aren't even 'cooked'. I love to balance out the robust taste of the walnut meat with this tangy pineapple salsa, paired with a garlicky creamy avocado sauce. Serves 2–4

130g walnuts

3 sun-dried tomatoes

1 scant teaspoon ground cumin

¼ teaspoon ground coriander

¼ teaspoon smoked paprika

pinch of cayenne pepper

½ tablespoon soy sauce or tamari

2 tablespoons extra virgin olive oil

2 little gem lettuces

FOR THE PINEAPPLE SALSA:

½ pineapple, peeled and diced

1 small yellow pepper, deseeded and diced

2 spring onions, sliced

1 small green chilli, deseeded and finely chopped

juice of 1 lime

20g fresh coriander, roughly chopped

FOR THE GARLICKY AVOCADO SAUCE:

1 avocado, peeled and stoned

1 tablespoon coconut cream or yogurt

1 garlic clove, crushed

juice of 1 lime

2 tablespoons extra virgin olive oil

2–4 tablespoons water

salt

1. Put the walnuts in a food processor or blender and blitz to a coarse rubble. Add the sun-dried tomatoes, spices, soy sauce or tamari and oil and pulse until it forms a crumbly 'meaty' texture.

2. For the pineapple salsa, put the pineapple and yellow pepper in a bowl. Add the spring onions and chilli. Squeeze over the lime juice and stir to combine before adding the coriander. Stir and set aside until needed.

3. For the avocado sauce, put the avocado flesh in a food processor or blender with the coconut cream or yogurt, garlic, lime juice and a pinch of salt and blend until smooth. While it's blending, gradually pour in the extra virgin olive oil until amalgamated before thinning out with a few tablespoons of water, depending on how thick you prefer it. Check for seasoning, adding a little more salt if necessary. Refrigerate until needed.

4. Separate the leaves from the little gem lettuces. Spread some avocado sauce in the centre of each lettuce leaf, spoon over a generous amount of walnut meat and top with the pineapple salsa. Eat, taco style.

BLACK BEAN TAQUITOS *with an* ENCHILADA SAUCE

Normally fried in excessive amounts of oil, taquitos aren't the healthiest Mexican option, which is why I've tried to cut down on the calorie count while still retaining that crucial crunch. Instead of going down the normal route, I've opted to brush each tortilla roll lightly with oil and toast them off in a dry pan... same effect, much less fat. The super-spicy enchilada sauce is what brings this harmonious plate of awesomeness together, making it one of my favourite (and frequent) week-night specials. Got guests? No worries. Just make them in batches and keep warm in a medium oven. Comfort. Food. Nailed. **Serves 2–4**

1 tablespoon olive oil, plus extra for brushing
1 onion, finely chopped
¼ fennel bulb, finely chopped
1 garlic clove
400g canned black beans, drained and rinsed
1 teaspoon ground cumin
1 rosemary sprig, finely chopped
½ vegetable stock cube
30ml soya cream (or other plant cream)
juice of ½ lime, plus extra to serve
4 x wholewheat tortillas
salt and freshly ground black pepper
sliced avocado and chopped fresh coriander, to serve

FOR THE ENCHILADA SAUCE:
1 tablespoon olive oil
1 onion, finely chopped
2 garlic cloves, crushed
1 red chilli, deseeded and finely chopped
1 teaspoon smoked paprika
¼ teaspoon cayenne pepper
½ tablespoon maple syrup
400g can plum tomatoes
juice of ½ lime

1. Heat the oil in a saucepan. Add the onion, season and sweat gently until translucent. Add the fennel. Cook until it begins to soften.
2. Add the garlic. Once fragrant, add the beans to the pan. Sprinkle over the cumin and rosemary, season and sauté for about 5 minutes.
3. Cover with water, add the stock cube and simmer for about 10 minutes until the liquid reduces significantly. Add the soya cream, stir to combine and cook for 1–2 minutes. Spritz over the lime juice, roughly mash, check for seasoning and set aside until needed.
4. For the enchilada sauce, heat the oil in a heavy-based saucepan. Add the onion to the pan, season and cook until translucent. Add the garlic, chilli, smoked paprika, cayenne and a splash of maple syrup and sauté for several minutes. Cook gently until fragrant before adding the tomatoes. Season and crush the tomatoes using the back of a spoon before simmering for 20 minutes.
5. Transfer to a food processor and blitz until smooth. Return to the pan, add the lime juice, check for seasoning and warm through.
6 Divide the black bean mixture between the tortillas and roll each into a tight cigar shape. Brush each taquito lightly with oil. Heat a large frying pan and toast each taquito all over until crispy and golden brown. Serve immediately with the enchilada sauce. Garnish with sliced avocado and coriander.

SPECIAL MEALS

CEVICHE-STYLE MUSHROOMS
KALE, APPLE *and* FENNEL SALAD
  with CANDIED PECAN TWIST
LAYERED NO-BAKE PESTO TART
COLCANNON
TENDERSTEM BROCCOLI with a ROMESCO SAUCE
RED PEPPER *and* SPINACH STROMBOLI
ROASTED BEETROOT and PUY LENTIL SALAD with
  an ORANGE, MAPLE and CAPER DRESSING
MAPLE ROASTED PARSNIPS
JERK-STYLE CAULIFLOWER STEAKS
JOLLOF RICE
ROASTED CAULIFLOWER FATTOUSH
ADUKI BEAN CASSEROLE
CHEESE and CREAMS 101
CANNELLINI BEAN STEW
  with a SOURED CASHEW CREAM
SAGE and POMEGRANATE MOCKTAIL FOR ONE

GLUTEN FREE **RAW**

CEVICHE-STYLE MUSHROOMS

Such a splendid summertime dish, these ceviche-style mushrooms are the perfect addition to any picnic or lunchtime spread. The citrus juice renders them so succulently soft it's almost as if they'd been cooked... a great way to fool your raw food fearing friends! I like to serve them in a variety of guises (they make great raw taco fillings but are equally lovely alongside my Quinoa Tabbouleh on page 85), so feel free to serve them as you see fit – although something tells me you'll end up eating them straight from the bowl. **Serves 2–4**

200g oyster mushrooms
juice and zest of 1 lime
1 spring onion, finely chopped
1 tablespoon extra virgin olive oil
30g fresh coriander, roughly chopped
sea salt and freshly ground black pepper

1. Tear the oyster mushrooms into small bite-size pieces and place in a bowl along with the lime zest and juice, spring onion, olive oil and some seasoning.
2. Stir to combine and set aside for about 30 minutes until the mushrooms absorb the flavours and become beautifully tender.
3. Stir the coriander through the mushrooms, taste for seasoning and serve.

VARIATION: For a version using chestnut mushrooms, simply slice the same weight of mushrooms and replace the lime zest and juice with lemon, use 1 finely sliced garlic clove instead of the spring onion, increase the oil to 2 tablespoons, and use parsley in place of the coriander.

KALE, APPLE *and* FENNEL SALAD *with* CANDIED PECAN TWIST

Salad, for me, is all about texture. Without a little crispness or crunch, it's simply not a pleasure to consume. I've had to endure one too many 'lettuce and tomato' offerings in my life to know that undressed leaves and a badly cut tomato simply don't cut it in the salad stakes... something I swore would never see the light of day in my own kitchen – bad salads begone! So, armed with just a handful of ingredients, I'm going to show you how to transform the familiar everyday salad into a 'wow' dish. Thanks to a little nutty sweetness, some mighty leaves, fragrant fennel and a simple apple, this is a salad to swoon over and not a soggy tomato in sight. **Serves 2**

2 tablespoons maple syrup
handful of pecans
1 small apple, cored
½ fennel bulb
1 tablespoon lemon juice
150g kale, stems removed and large pieces torn into smaller pieces
sea salt and freshly ground black pepper

FOR THE DRESSING:
1 heaped tablespoon wholegrain mustard
1 tablespoon red wine vinegar
1 tablespoon extra virgin olive oil
juice of ½ lime
½ tablespoon maple syrup

1. Put the syrup in a small heavy-based frying pan and heat gently until it begins to bubble. Toss in the pecans, sprinkle over a little sea salt and swirl until all the nuts are coated. Turn out immediately onto a clean board, sprinkle with a little more salt and leave to cool. Don't worry if they stick together – they will break apart easily when cool.
2. Cut the apples into rounds first, then finely slice into matchsticks. Shave the fennel as thinly as possible and put in a bowl with the apple. Squeeze over some lemon (or lime) juice to prevent them from browning.
3. Put the dressing ingredients in a jar and shake vigorously until emulsified. Pour half the dressing over the torn kale and massage into the leaves until they begin to soften. Set aside for 10 minutes to allow the kale to absorb the flavours and wilt.
4. Layer the kale over the apple matchsticks and fennel and spoon over the remaining dressing.
5. Break the candied pecans apart to separate and disperse evenly over the salad before serving.

LAYERED NO-BAKE PESTO TART

I'm not going to lie. When I first came across 'raw food' it kinda freaked me out. Even though I'd happily chow down on crudités and loved eating fruit, the thought of an entirely raw meal really did not appeal. Little did I know the immense cuisine that embodies this often much-maligned movement is vast and delicious, and after trying out a few dishes in raw food restaurants, such as Saf, I was officially hooked. Almost six years down the line and I'm forever experimenting with raw food in my own kitchen. This carrot, cashew and pesto combo makes for a great dinner party starter dish or entrée for a fancy lunch. The layers of textures and flavours are sure to trick your guests into thinking that you'd spent the day cooking instead of assembling... never a bad thing in my book. **Serves 4–6**

FOR THE CRUST:
2 small carrots, finely grated
70g walnuts
1 tablespoon mixed seeds
1 heaped tablespoon ground cumin
½ teaspoon paprika
½ tablespoon coconut oil
salt and freshly ground black pepper

FOR THE CASHEW CREAM:
130g soaked cashews (see page 120)
juice of ½ lemon
½ tablespoon coconut oil

FOR THE PESTO:
30g fresh basil leaves
30g spinach
2 tablespoons mixed nuts (walnuts and pecans work best)
juice of ½ lemon
1 small garlic clove
3 tablespoons extra virgin olive oil
3 tablespoons flaxseed oil

FOR THE CARROT SERVING SAUCE:
½ stoned Medjool date

1 tablespoon mixed seeds, such as pumpkin, sesame and sunflower, to serve

1. Squeeze out any excess juice from the grated carrots into a bowl – reserve this juice for the sauce. Put all the crust ingredients in a food processor or mini blender and blitz until it forms a fine rubble. Taste for seasoning and add a little more salt and pepper if necessary.

2. Line a 15cm tart tin or 225g loaf tin with baking parchment and press the crust evenly into the bottom. Freeze or refrigerate for 30 minutes to set.

3. Put all the cream ingredients in a food processor or blender with 50ml water and blitz until completely smooth, scraping down the sides as you go. This may take a while but persevere and it eventually becomes smooth. Check for seasoning, then pour the cream over the chilled carrot crust, reserving one heaped tablespoon for the sauce. Smooth out with a spatula and refrigerate for about 1 hour.

4. Put all the pesto ingredients in a food processor or mini blender and blend until coarse but spreadable. Taste for seasoning and add a touch more salt and pepper if necessary. Refrigerate for 20 minutes.

5. Put the reserved carrot juice in a food processor or blender, add the reserved tablespoon of cashew cream and the date and blitz until completely smooth.

6. Carefully lift the chilled tart out of the tin and ease it onto a serving board. Spoon over the pesto and carefully spread out using a spatula. Drizzle over the carrot sauce and adorn with crushed seeds and nuts.

COLCANNON

If you were ever in any doubt as to my origins, this plate says it all. Irish through and through – I live, breathe and dream in potatoes with this being my ultimate spud recipe... mash is my mecca and I bow at the temple of its greatness. I've used soya cream and milk in this recipe, which may polarise a few of you, so feel free to use any plant milk or cream of your choosing. And while I'm perfectly happy sitting down to a bowl of this on its own, it also goes brilliantly with a savoury pie or indeed as a topping to any potato-adorned casserole. Grub's up! **Serves 2–4 as a side**

4 large mashing potatoes (Desirée, Lady Balfour or Vivaldi), peeled and cut into small chunks
1 tablespoon olive oil
1 leek, sliced and rinsed
vegan margarine, for mashing
150g curly kale, washed, stems removed and roughly torn into small pieces
splash of soya milk (or other Plant Milk, see page 28)
1 heaped teaspoon Dijon mustard
splash of soya or oat cream
sea salt and freshly ground black pepper

1. Put the potatoes in a large saucepan, season with salt and cover with water. Clamp on the lid, bring to the boil, then reduce to a rolling simmer for about 15–20 minutes.

2. While the potatoes are cooking, heat the oil in a separate pan. Add the leeks to the pan, season and sweat until they begin to soften. Add a knob of vegan margarine, season and continue to cook gently until soft, ensuring they don't colour.

3. Add the kale to the pan, season generously and wilt. Set aside until needed.

4. Drain the potatoes and return to the pan. Add a knob of margarine, a splash of soya (or other plant) milk, season generously and mash. Stir through the Dijon mustard and a generous glug of soya cream before adding the leek/kale mixture. Stir to combine, check for seasoning and serve.

TENDERSTEM BROCCOLI *with a* ROMESCO SAUCE

Bringing the best out in broccoli is a continuing mission of mine. Not that I don't love it *au naturel* (because I really, really do) but there's nothing I take more pleasure in than accentuating its innate understated brilliance. I've discovered that broccoli is a pretty versatile little veg and can really take on bold flavours with aplomb, which is probably why it works so well with this uber smoky Spanish-style romesco sauce. Of course, you could totally use the sauce in other dishes too – it's particularly good in sarnies! – but if I want to impress, I know a platter of broccoli adorned with a dollop of romesco is bound to do the trick. You'll soon have your guests proclaiming broccoli's brilliance, too. **Serves 2–4 as a side**

1 red pepper, deseeded and quartered

1 red chilli

3 cherry tomatoes

1 large garlic clove, skin intact

50g toasted flaked almonds (see Note on toasting, page 86)

1 tablespoon olive oil

1 tablespoon red wine vinegar

250g tenderstem broccoli

sea salt and freshly ground black pepper

1. Heat a griddle pan over a high heat. Place the red pepper pieces, skin side down, on the pan along with the chilli, tomatoes and garlic. Cook until the skins are blackened. Wrap the pepper and chilli in cling film and set everything aside to cool.

2. Once cooled, the skins should easily peel away from the pepper and chilli. Pop the garlic from its skin and place everything in a food processor with the almonds, oil, vinegar and seasoning. Blend to a coarse paste.

3. Blanch or steam the broccoli and serve on a platter with the romesco sauce generously spooned over the top.

SPECIAL MEALS

107

RED PEPPER *and* SPINACH STROMBOLI

If you're after a quick dish, this really isn't it. It is, however, worth every minute of your effort. Stromboli is basically a gigantic pizza roll-up, which means you can just about fill it with anything you like. Be sure not to overfill, as it can make the dough less crispy and it's a heck of a lot messier to eat. **Serves 4–6**

200g plain white flour
1 teaspoon brown sugar
pinch of salt
1 scant teaspoon fast-action dried yeast
2 tablespoons olive oil, plus extra for drizzling
140ml lukewarm water

FOR THE SAUCE:

1–2 tablespoons olive oil
3 large garlic cloves, finely sliced
pinch of brown sugar
1 heaped teaspoon mixed Italian herbs
   or dried oregano
400g can plum tomatoes
splash of balsamic vinegar
sea salt and freshly ground black pepper

FOR THE FILLING:

1 large red pepper, deseeded and cut into
   eighths
350g spinach
50g grated vegan cheese or
   2 tablespoons nutritional yeast
   (optional, see page 10)

1. Sift the flour, sugar, salt and yeast onto a clean work surface. Whisk the oil and water together in a bowl or jug.

Make a well in the centre of the flour mixture and gradually add the water/oil. Use a whisk or fork to work the flour into the liquid, adding a little more liquid as you go until it forms a rough dough – you may not need all the water. **2.** Use your hands to work the dough into a rough ball shape and knead for 10 minutes until smooth and elastic.

3. Oil a large bowl and roll the dough ball in it to coat. Cover with cling film and set aside in a warm place to rise for 1 hour. **4.** For the sauce, heat a tablespoon of olive oil in a large heavy-based saucepan. Add the garlic and gently cook over a medium heat until fragrant. Add a touch of salt, the sugar and herbs. Gently sauté for a few minutes. **5.** Pour in the tomatoes and crush gently with the back of a spoon to break them up. Season and simmer for 20 minutes before adding the balsamic vinegar. Continue to simmer for 30–40 minutes or until thickened.

6. For the filling, heat a large griddle pan and add the red pepper pieces to the pan, skin-side down, and cook until charred. Wrap immediately in cling film and allow to cool for around 10 minutes before peeling off the skin – it should easily come away from the flesh. Slice the pieces of pepper into even strips. **7.** Bring a saucepan of water to the boil and add the spinach.

Gently wilt for about 5 minutes before removing with a slotted spoon and squeezing out any excess liquid. Transfer to a chopping board and mince to a pulp with a sharp knife. Season and set aside.

8. Once the dough has risen, turn it out onto a clean surface and knock the air out by kneading it for a minute or two. Flour a large baking tray and press or roll the dough out into a rough square shape, leaving a little room around the edge of the tray. Now preheat your oven to the highest setting – about 250°C/gas mark 9. **9.** Spoon over the cooled sauce and spread, leaving an inch of bare dough at the top – this will make sealing the stromboli easier. **10.** Distribute the spinach before dispersing the pepper strips evenly across the dough. At this stage you could also sprinkle over some grated vegan cheese or a little nutritional yeast. **11.** From the end closest to you, roll the stromboli carefully away from you, tucking the seam under when you reach the top. Move the stromboli diagonally across the baking sheet so it has room to expand and score the top with a floured knife. **12.** Bake for 15 minutes or until completely crisp and golden before transferring to a serving board. Cut into thick, even pieces for a great communal party dish.

ROASTED BEETROOT *and* PUY LENTIL SALAD *with an* ORANGE, MAPLE *and* CAPER DRESSING

If you're after an eye-poppingly good salad, then you happen to be in luck. Positively bursting with goodness, this has got a bit of everything... protein, thanks to the lentils, vitamin C in the form of leafy greens, but really it's all about that succulent salad dressing, and, of course, those blood pressure reducing slices of oven-roasted beetroot. **Serves 2**

4 small beetroots, peeled and sliced
1 tablespoon olive oil
1 tablespoon red wine vinegar
200g rocket
1 tablespoon mixed seeds
sea salt and freshly ground black pepper

FOR THE PUY LENTILS:
250g cooked Puy lentils
4 sun-dried tomatoes, chopped
juice of ½ lemon
handful of chopped fresh flat-leaf parsley
extra virgin olive oil, to drizzle

FOR THE DRESSING:
1 tablespoon Dijon mustard
juice of ½ orange
2 tablespoons red wine vinegar
1 tablespoon maple syrup
1 tablespoon capers, minced

1. Preheat the oven to 200°C/gas mark 6. Put the beetroot slices on a baking dish, drizzle with the olive oil and red wine vinegar, season, cover with foil and roast for 45 minutes or until soft. Set aside until needed.
2. For the Puy lentils, put the lentils and sun-dried tomatoes in a large bowl. Season generously, then add the lemon juice, parsley and a drizzle of oil and stir.
3. Whisk the dressing ingredients together until they emulsify. Dress the rocket leaves with a bit of the dressing and divide between two bowls.
4. Scatter over the Puy lentil mixture and top with the roasted beetroot. Drizzle over the remaining dressing and finish with mixed seeds.

MAPLE ROASTED PARSNIPS

A simple side with the slightest twist, these roasted parsnips with a sugary maple kick are just the ticket to liven up any traditional lunch. The syrup renders them deliciously sticky, bringing to life that deep root vegetable flavour, all perfectly accentuated by those most distinctively earthy herbs, sage and rosemary. For me, the merest waft of sage in all its pungent, aromatic glory cannot fail to conjure up childhood memories awaiting that 'roast', and just because I'm vegan doesn't mean I can't still indulge – albeit without the meat. But who needs meat anyway, with these magnificent parsnips stealing the Sunday lunch show? Pass the gravy, please.

Serves 2–4

4 large parsnips
25g fresh sage, finely chopped
10g fresh rosemary, finely chopped
1 tablespoon rapeseed oil
3 tablespoons maple syrup
handful of hazelnuts, crushed
sea salt and freshly ground black pepper

1. Preheat the oven to 200°C/gas mark 6.
2. Halve each parsnip and slice lengthways. Transfer to a baking dish.
3. Add the herbs to the parsnip along with the oil and 2 tablespoons of the maple syrup. Season generously with salt and pepper and roast for about 30–35 minutes.
4. Drizzle over the remaining maple syrup, season with more salt and roast for a further 10–15 minutes until golden, glossy and perfectly cooked.
5. Heat a dry frying pan and toast the crushed hazelnuts over a medium heat until they become fragrant and slightly crunchy.
6. Serve the parsnips with a smattering of the toasted hazelnuts over the top.

JERK-STYLE CAULIFLOWER STEAKS

I love experimenting with spices and injecting a lot of flavour into ingredients that have very little. Cauliflower is one such vegetable, subtle enough to absorb all that luscious marinade while still retaining some necessary bite. Steaming the 'steaks' when they first go in the oven ensures the spices seep into every crevice but crucially, it is their griddle pan finish that adds that necessary finesse to the dish. Serve alongside some Jollof Rice (see page 115) for a double spice hit or go simple with a dressed green salad for a delicious midweek meal. These steaks also work well served with herbed bulgar wheat and wilted spinach.

Serves 4

1 medium cauliflower

FOR THE MARINADE:
35g fresh coriander
thumb-size piece of fresh ginger
1 scotch bonnet
2 garlic cloves
1 tablespoon olive oil
½ tablespoon maple syrup
1 teaspoon ground cumin
½ teaspoon ground coriander
½ teaspoon paprika
1 teaspoon smoked paprika
¼ teaspoon cayenne pepper
juice of ½ lime
sea salt and freshly ground black pepper

1. Preheat the oven to 200°C/gas mark 6.
2. Place all the marinade ingredients into a food processor or mini blender and blitz until coarse but spreadable.
3. Remove the leaves from around the cauliflower, but don't remove the bulb at the bottom, as this is what will keep your steaks intact. Halve the cauliflower and, working from the cut side out, slice each steak around 1½cm thick... you will probably only get two full steaks from each half but you can roast the remaining florets in the same way.
4. Generously brush the steaks with the marinade. If you want to do this ahead of time, you can leave them to marinate in the fridge until you need them.
5. Place the steaks on a roasting tray and loosely cover with foil. Roast for 15–20 minutes before removing the foil for a further 10 minutes, turning once.
6. Heat a griddle pan to a medium-high heat and finish the steaks off in the pan to mark/sear on both sides. Serve with your chosen accompaniment.

JOLLOF RICE

If I told you my introduction to jollof rice came via the TV, would you judge me a little or a lot? Suffice to say, as soon as I witnessed that steaming pot of goodness in all its tomato-ey glory I just knew I had to recreate it in my own kitchen. Of course, this is very much my own (anglicised) spin on things so if you're looking for an authentic version of what I now realise to be a staple national dish for much of West Africa, this probably isn't it. What it is, however, is a pot of unmatchable comfort complete with spice, carbs and all that wholesome good stuff that makes you smile contentedly after consuming. I'll take those high fives now please. **Serves 2-4**

1 tablespoon of olive oil
1 large onion, finely chopped
3 large garlic cloves, finely sliced
thumb-size piece of fresh ginger, peeled and grated
1 teaspoon paprika
¼ teaspoon cayenne pepper
¼ teaspoon ground coriander
400g can plum tomatoes
1 teaspoon sugar or palm sugar
1 scotch bonnet, sliced
200g brown rice
1 vegetable stock cube
large bunch of fresh coriander, roughly chopped
sea salt and freshly ground black pepper

1. Heat the oil in a large heavy-based pan. Add the onion, season, and sweat for several minutes until it begins to soften. Add the garlic and let it infuse for several minutes before adding the ginger. Cook for about 10 minutes until the onion is completely soft.
2. Add the spices and fry for a few minutes. Pour in the tomatoes, stir and gently simmer for 5 or so minutes until the tomatoes are soft enough to crush with the back of a spoon.
3. Add the sugar and scotch bonnet and season. Simmer for a further 15 minutes until the sauce has reduced and the tomatoes are almost completely smooth.
4. Rinse the rice and add it to the pan. Fill the empty tomato can with water and also add to the pan along with the vegetable stock cube. Simmer for about 1 hour or until the rice has absorbed all the liquid and is completely cooked. Try not to stir it too much but do ensure it isn't sticking to bottom – a fork works best. You may need to add a touch more water but as the dish should be reasonably dry, avoid adding too much. The rice will eventually absorb all the sauce.
5. Gently fork the coriander through the rice, reserving some for sprinkling on top when serving.

ROASTED CAULIFLOWER FATTOUSH

Salads don't have to be dull and boring. All they need is a little tender loving care (and perhaps the odd dash of spice) to really bring them to life. Here, I'm talking 'in yer face' roasted cauliflower florets paired with toasted pitta pieces and a creamy tahini dressing that will end your limp leaf memories and catapult you into what I've dubbed '21st Century Eating'. That's where we have our cake (or in this case, salad) and eat it... flavour, texture and freshness combined – there's very little not to like about this recipe. So much so, I'd happily serve it for lunch, dinner and even at parties – it never fails to get a bounty of enthusiastic 'mmm's and 'wow's. Now, when's the last time you heard that said about a salad? **Serves 2–4**

1 small cauliflower, broken into small florets
1 little gem lettuce
5–6 cherry tomatoes, halved
⅓ large cucumber, peeled, deseeded and cut into half moons
5–6 radishes, roughly chopped
2 pittas, toasted
30g fresh flat-leaf parsley
30g fresh coriander
15g fresh mint
sea salt and freshly ground black pepper

FOR THE CAULIFLOWER MARINADE:
1 teaspoon smoked paprika, plus extra to serve
1 teaspoon ground cumin
½ teaspoon ground cinnamon
½ teaspoon chilli powder
½ teaspoon allspice
pinch of cayenne pepper
juice of ½ lime
1 teaspoon agave nectar
½ tablespoon olive oil

FOR THE CHILLI SALAD DRESSING:
1 teaspoon chilli paste from a jar (eg. sambal oelek)
1 tablespoon red wine vinegar
1 teaspoon agave nectar
juice of ½ lime
3 tablespoons olive oil

FOR THE TAHINI DRESSING:
3 tablespoons hummus
2 tablespoons tahini
1 teaspoon agave nectar
juice of ½ lime

1. Preheat the oven to 200°C/ gas mark 6. Place the cauliflower florets in a baking dish. Whisk the marinade ingredients together, along with some seasoning, to form a smooth paste and pour over the cauliflower florets. Toss together until everything is coated and bake for about 45 minutes or until nicely browned.

2. Put the lettuce, tomatoes, cucumber and radishes in a large bowl. Whisk the chilli dressing ingredients together and pour about one-third over the salad. Mix together.

3. Lightly toast or griddle the pittas and cut into triangular bite-size pieces. Drizzle over about one-third of the chilli dressing and add to the salad bowl.

4. Finely chop the parsley, coriander and mint together on a clean chopping board and sprinkle two thirds over the salad bowl ingredients. Gently mix.

5. Whisk the tahini sauce ingredients together with 60ml water until smooth, adding more water if necessary.

6. Remove the roasted cauliflower from the oven and lightly season with some sea salt. Add to the salad and gently toss. Serve in a bowl, drizzle over the tahini dressing and a smattering of smoked paprika, and garnish with the remaining parsley, coriander and mint.

ADUKI BEAN CASSEROLE

Gratin casseroles are the way forward in my opinion. No need to boil and mash potatoes when you can slice them thinly and bake until golden in the oven. There is a rather crazy mix of flavourings happening in this particular dish – miso, marmite and coconut milk – but it does amalgamate to form a lovely and richly layered sauce that bubbles up around the edges of the sweet potato slices, rendering them perfectly crisp and 100 per cent delicious. **Serves 2–4**

1 tablespoon olive oil, plus a little extra
  for the sweet potato
2 onions, finely chopped
1 carrot, finely chopped
2 large garlic cloves, sliced
1 teaspoon chilli flakes, plus a little
  extra for the sweet potato
½ tablespoon red wine vinegar
thumb-size piece of fresh ginger,
  peeled and grated, plus a little extra
  for the sweet potato
1 tablespoon tomato purée
150ml coconut milk
½ vegetable stock cube
225g canned aduki beans
1 teaspoon Marmite
1 heaped teaspoon miso paste
100g frozen peas
1 large sweet potato, peeled and finely
  sliced into rounds
sea salt and freshly ground
  black pepper

1. Preheat the oven to 180°C/gas mark 4.

2. Heat the oil in a heavy-based saucepan. Add the onion, carrot, garlic and chilli flakes. Season and sweat until the onion becomes translucent. Add the red wine vinegar and cook over a high heat until it evaporates.

3. Reduce the heat and grate in the ginger before adding the tomato purée, coconut milk and stock cube. Simmer until the vegetables are soft.

4. Drain and rinse the aduki beans and add to the pan along with the Marmite and miso. Simmer gently for several minutes before tumbling in the frozen peas. Season and simmer gently until the peas are heated through. Transfer to a casserole dish.

5. Toss the sweet potato slices with a little olive oil, some grated ginger, chilli flakes and salt. Line the top of the casserole with the sweet potato, overlapping to ensure it all fits in. Cover with foil and bake for about 30 minutes before removing the foil and cooking for a further 20 minutes or until the topping is crispy and golden.

CHEESES
and CREAMS 101

There are a lot of vegan cheeses out there, but if you fancy trying out some homemade versions, help is at hand. Don't expect the flavour to be quite as full on as their dairy counterparts; relish their plant-based richness instead. I'm now at the stage where I no longer compare, and I can simply enjoy them for what they are. However, I have been told my soured cashew cream is better than the real thing!

The basic component for any vegan cheese or cream is soaked nuts – I mainly rely on cashews, almonds and macadamias because they render the smoothest (and most unctuous) texture. And once you have the basic recipes down pat, you can then play around with flavours and add-ins... anything from herbs and spices through to chopped peppers, sun-dried tomatoes, olives and more.

Let's start with the soaking. Place your chosen nuts in a bowl, cover with filtered water and set aside for at least 6 hours or better still, overnight. Feel free to change the water halfway through. Once they are plump, drain and rinse the nuts and, depending on what you are making, place them in your chosen kitchen gadget... I normally use my blender for creams and my food processor for cheeses.

What you add to your nuts will determine how thick the result will be – the more liquid you add, the runnier it will be. For this reason I try to add the least amount of liquid to my cheeses because I prefer them to be as firm as possible. Seasoning is crucial but you don't want to overdo the salt, as the nuts will simply absorb it and become overpoweringly bitter...

so remember to add a little at a time. My go-to ingredients for any savoury cheese or cream is lemon juice and cider vinegar, and maybe a touch of Dijon mustard. You could also add some nutritional yeast if you like but it's not something I use frequently, if at all, because I prefer a cleaner flavour. It's also worth noting that adding nutritional yeast will mean these cheeses are not gluten-free.

For sweet creams, I almost always add agave nectar or maple syrup and maybe a dash of vanilla too. You could also play around with different extracts, spices or add-ins, including almond, cinnamon, cacao or my favourite... orange blossom water.

Baked cheeses will be much more robust in flavour and therefore take a little more preparation. Once blended they will have to be strained over a fine-mesh sieve overnight to remove any excess liquid before being baked the next day. I've included a recipe for a basic Baked Almond Cheese that is almost akin to a feta – crumbly and mouth-coatingly moreish – spread it on crackers or crumble it through a Greek-style salad. Homemade 'cheese' a go-go!

BAKED ALMOND CHEESE
Serves 4–6

100g blanched almonds
juice of 1 large lemon
25ml extra virgin olive oil
1 teaspoon cider vinegar
1 teaspoon agave nectar, plus extra for drizzling
1 heaped teaspoon salt
¼ teaspoon freshly ground black pepper

1. Place all the ingredients in a food processor or blender and blend until completely smooth, adding a tablespoon of water if necessary and scraping down the sides from time to time.
2. Check for seasoning – it may need a touch more salt and/or lemon.
3. Transfer to a nut milk bag or muslin cloth and strain over a fine-mesh sieve overnight to remove any excess liquid – don't worry if there isn't much in the bowl.
4. Preheat the oven to 180°C/gas mark 4. Form the 'cheese' into a rough ball. Coat in a little more extra virgin olive oil and transfer to an ovenproof bowl. Bake for 45 minutes. Remove from the oven and leave to cool.
5. Serve with a generous drizzle of agave nectar, crushed walnuts, crackers and a chilled glass of white wine. Summer dining. Sorted.

SOURED CASHEW CREAM
Serves 4–6

110g soaked cashews (see opposite)
1 tablespoon cider vinegar
1 tablespoon lemon juice
pinch of salt
½ tablespoon coconut oil
50ml filtered water

1. Place the soaked cashews, cider vinegar, lemon juice, salt, coconut oil and water in a food processor or high-speed blender and blitz until completely smooth and creamy. It will go through several stages... grainy, coarse and finally smooth. Be patient and you will soon achieve the desired consistency. Check seasoning and refrigerate until needed.
2. Serve alongside a variety of Mexican dishes or dollop onto jacket potatoes with a generous sprinkling of chives.

SWEET CREAMS
Serves 4–6

100g soaked cashews or almonds
2 tablespoons agave nectar or maple syrup
150–300ml filtered water (use 150ml for a thicker cream and 300ml for a more pourable variety)
pinch of salt

1. Blend the ingredients as in step 1 of Baked Almond Cheese, opposite.
2. Once smooth, you can add a variety of flavourings including vanilla extract, ground cinnamon or even a heaped tablespoon of raw cacao powder. Alternatively, serve *au naturel* with your chosen dessert or breakfast (see Stuffed Baked Apples, page 33).

CANNELLINI BEAN STEW *with a* SOURED CASHEW CREAM

The tarragon, sage and dill in this stew make a wondrous combination that is both fragrant and earthy... but nothing can top the soured cashew cream side that gives this dish something of a Bavarian feel. This is hearty, wholesome fare intended solely to warm those cockles. Nothing fancy, just simple food with some interesting flavours and a decent dose of nutritional goodness too. **Serves 2–3**

1 tablespoon olive oil
1 onion, roughly chopped
1 celery stick, roughly chopped
1 small head of broccoli, stalk chopped and broken into florets
2 large garlic cloves, finely sliced
5 chantenay carrots, halved
10g fresh tarragon, finely chopped
10g fresh sage, finely chopped
10g fresh dill, finely chopped, plus extra to serve
1 vegetable stock cube
50g green beans, topped, tailed and cut into thirds
2 tablespoons plain flour
400g can cannellini beans, drained and rinsed
1 tablespoon capers, minced, plus extra to serve
handful of kale
pinch or 2 of nutritional yeast (see page 10), to serve
Soured Cashew Cream (see left)
sea salt and freshly ground black pepper

1. Heat the oil in a heavy-based saucepan. Add the onion, celery and broccoli stalk to the pan. Season and sweat until they begin to soften. Add the garlic and sweat further until the vegetables become translucent.
2. Add the carrots and herbs to the pan, season, cover and gently sauté until the carrots begin to soften. Cover completely with water, add the stock cube and gently simmer for about 20 minutes.
3. Add the green beans to the pan and simmer for 5 minutes. Whisk the flour with a little water to make a paste and add to the pan. Let the sauce thicken, then add the cannellini beans, broccoli florets and capers. Add 2–3 heaped tablespoons of the soured cream and gently heat.
4. Stir through the kale and allow it to gently wilt for several minutes.
5. Check for seasoning and serve the stew in warmed bowls. Garnish each bowl with a tablespoon of cream, a smattering of dill, capers and a pinch or two of nutritional yeast.

SAGE *and* POMEGRANATE MOCKTAIL *for* ONE

I'm partial to a cocktail but sometimes I want to forgo the alcohol for something a little healthier and less boozy. Adding herbs to mocktails lends that necessary flavour dimension that could almost fool you into thinking you're drinking the real thing. Here, I opted for sage but this also works really well with thyme leaves. Just be sure not to break the herbs up too much when you muddle or else you'll find a few unpleasant leafy remnants in your drink – a few turns is all it takes to release the wonderful aromas and oils. Truth be told, sipping on one of these has become my favourite Friday night pastime – I'm almost over alcohol entirely... almost. **Serves 1**

5–6 fresh sage leaves
½ lime, halved
juice of ½ pink grapefruit
juice of ½ orange
juice of ½ pomegranate
1 teaspoon agave nectar
several ice cubes

TO SERVE:
crushed ice
pomegranate seeds

1. Place the sage leaves in the bottom of a thick-rimmed glass or cocktail shaker along with the lime. Muddle the two together by using a cocktail muddler or similar instrument by pressing firmly and in a clockwise motion several times until the oils are released from both.
2. Add the grapefruit, orange and pomegranate juice, agave and ice, along with a splash of water, and shake firmly in a cocktail shaker until you can no longer hear the ice clattering against the sides and the outside of the shaker has frosted.
3. Fill a small glass with crushed ice and pour in the mocktail. Garnish with pomegranate seeds.

SWEET STUFF

BLISS BALLS 101
WHOLEMEAL 'BUTTERMILK' SCONES
APPLES with a CARAMEL DIPPING SAUCE
HOKEY POKEY
FRUIT 'N' NUT TRUFFLE SQUARES
GLUTEN-FREE ORANGE POLENTA CAKE
TWO WAYS with BANANA BREAD
CARROT *and* WALNUT CAKE
SPICED MOLASSES BUNDT BREAD
STICKY BOURBON BAKLAVA
MATCHA and PECAN COOKIES
BEETROOT *and* LEMON CUPCAKES
MACADAMIA and BLUEBERRY CREAM PIE
MINT CHOC AVOCADO PUD
COCONUT RICE PUDDING
SIMPLE STRAWBERRY GALETTE
BANOFFEE PIE
SIMPLE OATY COOKIES
SMUGGLERS' HOT COCOA with
SWEETENED WHIPPED COCONUT CREAM

BLISS BALLS 101

If you haven't heard of bliss balls yet, you are in for a serious treat my friends! These candy-like balls of goodness are my ultimate go-to snack and I can't tell you how much I love playing about with the seemingly endless flavour combinations... literally anything goes, so view these recipes as a guide and go get creative in the kitchen yourself. The only rules that really apply here are which dried fruit you prefer and which nut variety happens to float yer boat – the rest is really up to you. To get you started I've divided my bliss ball tutorial into the four main dried fruits I use most frequently myself... raisins, apricots, figs and dates. Each one will render a slightly different texture and you can also combine the dried fruits too – for example, raisins and dates work particularly well together. On the nut front I usually opt for soft nuts such as pecans and walnuts, as well as flaked and ground almonds, but you can absolutely go for cashews, whole almonds, hazelnuts, pistachios and more – just be sure to soak them first because they tend to be a little bit tougher.

To add depth I try to ensure there are always at least three elements in my mixture... think citrus zest, spices (cinnamon, cardamom, allspice, ginger), coconut oil, powders (maca, hemp, spirulina, chlorella), extracts (rose water, orange blossom water, vanilla extract), nut butters (peanut, almond, tahini and cashew), whole nuts, oats and seeds (sesame, pumpkin, sunflower, hemp), which all lend an added layer of flavour to proceedings. More often than not though, the simpler the better, so try not to overload the mixture with too many add-ins or the individual flavours will most likely get lost. For me, it's all about accentuating one or two ingredients, not masking them in an abundance of spices and powders.

Generally speaking, dates and raisins can handle more robust ingredients like cocoa, maca and peanut butter while the prunes and apricots have a more gentle sweetness that goes particularly well with fresh citrus notes, as well as almonds, pistachios and, that most delicate of extracts (and my personal fave)... rose water. It's all about balance, and you may come up with a few duds in the process, but that's certainly half the fun. Not only do they taste amazing, they also make wonderful gifts – once you've shaped them into balls, toss them in a mixture of coatings such as desiccated coconut, sesame seeds, cocoa (or raw cacao) powder, crushed nuts or anything that basically makes them look pretty. Bag 'em and hand them out at will, *et voilà*, you've just made an impression with little to no effort. Truthfully though, they rarely make it out of my kitchen. Unless you devour them all immediately, these balls will keep for up to 1 week in the fridge.

CHOCOLATEY RAISIN BITES

To get the best consistency from raisins, always soak them. This chocolate, peanut and raisin mixture will be sticky and dense but very pliable. If you wanted to add a nutritional boosting powder here, maca would be an excellent choice, giving the balls a lovely malty quality – but be sure not to overdo it... a scant teaspoon will suffice.
Makes 10–12 balls

100g rolled oats
150g soaked raisins
3 tablespoons 100% peanut butter
2 heaped tablespoons good-quality cocoa (or raw cacao) powder, plus extra for dusting
1 heaped teaspoon maca (optional)
1 teaspoon good-quality vanilla extract
pinch of sea salt

1. Place the oats in a food processor or blender and blend to a fine powder. Add the remaining ingredients and blitz until it becomes sand-like but forms into balls when squeezed. If you are using a high speed blender, you'll need to use a spatula to move the dough around.
2. Turn the mixture out onto a chopping board and shape into equal-size balls – I find that ½ tablespoon is the perfect amount. Leave to set in the fridge for at least 3 hours (preferably overnight) and dust with cocoa powder before serving. Alternatively, press into a loaf tin, dust with cocoa powder and cut into squares once set.

ZESTY APRICOT BALLS

I love how bright and zingy the apricot flavour is here, especially when paired with any kind of citrus fruit, and the soft, chewy texture is quite literally out of this world. And because dried apricots have that slightly Middle Eastern feel to them anyway it makes perfect sense to match them with almonds. Coconut is never far from my mind and I couldn't think of a better accompaniment to the lime than this. **Makes 10–12 balls**

200g soft dried apricots
200g flaked almonds
100g desiccated coconut, plus more for rolling
grated zest of 1 lime

1. Put all the ingredients in a food processor or mini blender and blitz until thoroughly smooth and combined. Again, if using a high-speed blender, you will need to scrape the sides down frequently and move the mixture around to prevent it from sticking to the blades and burning out your motor.
2. Turn the mixture out onto a chopping board and shape into equal-size balls – I find that ½ tablespoon is the perfect amount. Roll each ball in desiccated coconut before refrigerating. These balls will never become completely firm but their zingy, squishy interior is their biggest selling point.

PISTACHIO AND PUMPKIN SEED FIGGY BALLS

Dried figs are something we should probably all eat more of. Here I've partnered them with pumpkin seeds and pistachio. These energy bites are full of fibre and just enough sweetness to make them feel like a treat. The rose water is the star element that brings the core ingredients together, adding just enough intrigue to keep you coming back for more. **Makes 10–12 balls**

90g pistachios
50g pumpkin seeds
100g dried figs
1 teaspoon rose water
1 heaped teaspoon hemp powder (optional)

1. Blitz or crush 40g of the pistachios in a food processor or mini blender and set them aside for coating.
2. Put the remaining 50g pistachios and the pumpkin seeds in a food processor or mini blender and blitz to a fine rubble.
3. Remove the stalk at the top of each dried fig, halve and add to the processor along with the rose water and hemp powder, if using. Blitz thoroughly until it forms a large sticky, pliable dough.
4. Turn out onto a chopping board and shape into equal-size balls – I find that ½ tablespoon is the perfect amount. Roll each ball in the crushed pistachios. Repeat until all the dough is used and then refrigerate for at least 1 hour but ideally overnight.

CARAMEL BONBONS

Medjool dates lend the perfect of amount of sweetness and chew and are my go-to soft fruit for bliss balls. This recipe is perhaps my favourite – they remind me of the chewy toffee bonbons I used to love so much as a child. The added raw chocolate coating is the cherry on the icing on the cake. **Makes 8 balls**

4 stoned Medjool dates
3 heaped tablespoons ground almonds
1 heaped tablespoon desiccated coconut
1 heaped tablespoon almond butter
crushed cacao nibs, for rolling

FOR THE CHOCOLATE COATING:
1 tablespoon coconut oil
2 tablespoons raw cacao or cocoa powder
1 teaspoon agave nectar

1. Put all the ingredients in a food processor or mini blender and blitz until it forms a smooth, sticky rubble.
2. Turn out onto a chopping board and shape into equal-size balls – I find that ½ tablespoon is the perfect amount. Set aside.
3. For the coating, melt the coconut oil in a small saucepan before whisking in the cacao and agave until smooth.
4. Toss each ball in the chocolate coating and place on a small dish lined with baking parchment. Sprinkle over the crushed cacao nibs and refrigerate for several hours or until the chocolate firms.

TRADITIONAL WHOLEMEAL 'BUTTERMILK' SCONES

Living in Cornwall, I'm surrounded by scones that I can't eat. Sometimes I feel like it's tantamount to torture, which is why I had to find a solution to meet my frequent scone-hankering needs. Thankfully this wholemeal vegan 'buttermilk' version is just the ticket to keep those moments of weakness at bay, and has quickly become my go-to recipe whenever the urge takes me to treat myself to afternoon tea. The only other perennial scone quandary is... 'cream' or jam first? **Serves 6–8**

175ml soya milk (or other suitable Plant Milk, see page 28)
1 teaspoon cider vinegar
1 teaspoon vanilla extract
200g wholemeal flour
100g plain flour
1 teaspoon baking powder
½ teaspoon bicarbonate of soda
pinch of salt
3 tablespoons caster sugar or 1 tablespoon agave nectar
85g cold vegan margarine

1. Preheat the oven to 220°C/gas mark 7.

2. Pour the soya milk into a jug and add the cider vinegar and vanilla extract (and agave, if using). Set aside to curdle.

3. Put the flours in a large mixing bowl along with the baking powder, bicarbonate of soda, salt and sugar (if using), and gently incorporate.

4. Lightly rub the margarine through the flour mix using your fingertips until combined. Make a well in the centre and add the soya milk mixture. Quickly incorporate using a metal spoon until it just comes together – the mixture will be quite wet.

5. Generously flour a surface and your hands and turn the dough out onto it. Very lightly knead the dough (turning it only several times) and flatten into a rough oval shape about 4cm thick.

6. Flour a round scone cutter and, depending on what size you prefer, press out as many scone shapes as possible before reshaping the dough and repeating until all or most of the dough is used.

7. Dust each scone with flour before baking for 10–15 minutes, depending on your oven.

8. Transfer to a wire rack and, once cool, slice and serve with Whipped Coconut Cream (see page 154) and Chia Jam (see page 40). The scones will keep for 3–5 days in a sealed container.

APPLES *with* a CARAMEL DIPPING SAUCE

Dates are magnificent, don't you think? Full of calcium and fibre, and so sweet they could almost be candy. While there's nothing new about 'date caramel' this is my favourite combination (the salt is *crucial*). Pressing it through the sieve is entirely optional. I prefer my dip/spread to be uber smooth, but you do sacrifice some nutrients in the process. It's a compromise I'm willing to make because it renders the caramel wonderfully smooth. In fact, forget dipping apples into it, why not spread this baby on toast and be done with it – sounds like a winning snack to me. **Serves 2–4**

6 stoned Medjool dates
5 tablespoons water
1 teaspoon vanilla extract
generous pinch of salt
2–4 apples, sliced

1. Soak the dates in some water for about 10 minutes to soften, then drain.
2. Put them in a food processor or mini blender with the 5 tablespoons water, vanilla extract and salt and blend until smooth.
3. Press through a fine-mesh sieve to separate any remaining skin and refrigerate until needed.
4. Serve with sliced apple for a healthy treat.

HOKEY POKEY

I'm fairly certain this is the stuff that dentist's nightmares are made of. Full of sugar, unbearably crunchy and teeth-destroyingly chewy with not one ounce of nutritional value – all in all, the antithesis of everything we are currently encouraged to eat. But it does have one overriding redeeming quality, which is that it tastes SO DAMN GOOD! Because it's something I only make a few times a year, I'll live with the minor dietary (and dental) consequences for the momentary thrill of biting into this very British confectionery that will always have a special place in my heart. **Serves 6–8**

200g caster sugar
4 tablespoons golden syrup
1½ teaspoons bicarbonate of soda

1. Line a large chopping board with baking parchment.
2. Mix the sugar and golden syrup in a saucepan until combined.
3. Heat until it begins to bubble, then simmer for a further 3–5 minutes until golden and smooth – do not stir!
4. Take the pan off the heat and quickly whisk in the bicarbonate of soda. Turn out immediately onto the parchment and leave it to cool completely.
5. Once set, break into pieces using a hammer or very sharp knife. Store in a container for up to a week.

TIP: Melt some dark chocolate in a bain marie or a heatproof bowl over a saucepan of simmering water. Drizzle the melted chocolate over the broken shards of hokey pokey, then leave to set.

FRUIT 'N' NUT TRUFFLES

Something shifts when you turn vegan. All that sugary sweet confectionery gets replaced with high-quality dark chocolate full of antioxidants and other 'good-for-you' ingredients. Don't ask me how but your palate will change – even if all you can think about right now is a good ol' bar of Dairy Milk... or whatever your chocolate vice may be. I remember being partial to the odd bar of 'Fruit and Nut' (that crunch and chew just did it for me) although in hindsight I now realise it was more to do with the dried fruit and crunchy nut inclusion rather than the gluey 'chocolate' that encased it. So, in an attempt to relive my youth (it won't have been the first time) I embarked on a quest to put my favourite flavours (and textures) into a wholly vegan truffle using only the best ingredients and with the added bonus of being kinda good for you... and you know what? It works! 'Fruit and Nut' quest complete.

Serves 4–6

1 tablespoon coconut oil
100g dark chocolate chips
2 tablespoons tahini
1 tablespoon agave nectar
1 teaspoon vanilla extract
pinch of salt
30g hazelnuts, roughly chopped
30g dried cranberries
cocoa powder, for dusting

1. Put the coconut oil into a small saucepan set over a medium heat and once melted add the chocolate chips. Let the chocolate melt slowly over a low heat before adding the tahini, agave, vanilla extract and salt. Gently whisk together to fully incorporate all the ingredients.

2. Add the hazelnuts and cranberries to the melted chocolate and fold through to evenly disperse.

3. Line a 225g loaf tin with baking parchment and pour in the chocolate mix, smoothing with the back of a spatula. Refrigerate overnight.

4. Remove the chocolate slab from the tin and cut into large squares or sticks. Dust each piece in cocoa powder. Best kept refrigerated and will keep for up to a fortnight.

GLUTEN-FREE ORANGE POLENTA CAKE

Nothing beats the smell of this deeply sensuous cake baking in the oven. It's enough to send me doo-lally and want to scoff the entire thing in a millisecond. But (but, but, but!) patience is the key here because you'll have to wait until it's completely cool before slathering it in the unctuous cashew frosting that sends this cake from merely fantastic into the baking stratosphere – yes, it really is that good. What makes it all the more satisfying is the sheer simplicity of its construction (you really don't need to be a master baker to accomplish this one) and the über crumbly texture, which makes it the perfect accompaniment to a traditional cuppa – take it from me, this pairing is absolute, unadulterated bliss. So, what are you waiting for? Get the kettle on, it's time for tea and cake. **Serves 8–10**

120g polenta
80g ground almonds
100g gram flour
1 teaspoon bicarbonate of soda
zest and juice of 2 blood oranges
100ml olive oil
100ml agave nectar
½ teaspoon orange extract
100ml soya yogurt
40g crushed pistachios, to decorate

FOR THE CASHEW FROSTING:
150g cashews, soaked for at least 6 hours (see page 120)
100ml agave nectar
juice and zest of ½ orange
½ teaspoon orange extract
1 heaped teaspoon coconut oil
2–3 tablespoons water

1. Preheat the oven to 170°C/gas mark 3 and grease and line a 15cm cake tin.

2. First, make the frosting. Drain and rinse the cashews and blend in a food processor or high-speed blender with the agave, orange juice and zest, orange extract, coconut oil and 2 tablespoons of the water. Scrape down the sides frequently until it becomes completely smooth, adding a little more water if necessary. The frosting will go through several stages; nutty, coarse and eventually silky smooth. You really do have to persevere to achieve the perfect frosting consistency, but don't take a shortcut by adding too much liquid. Keep blending and it will eventually become a shadow of its former cashew self. Refrigerate until needed.

3. Mix the polenta, ground almonds, gram flour and bicarbonate of soda together in a large bowl. Stir through the blood orange zest to ensure it is evenly distributed.

4. In a separate bowl, vigorously whisk together the oil, blood orange juice, agave, orange extract and yogurt.

5. Make a well in the centre of the flour and pour in the orange and olive oil mixture. Fold gently and transfer to the prepared cake tin.

6. Bake for 30–35 minutes. Check whether the cake is cooked by inserting a skewer to see if it comes out clean.

7. Once baked, leave to cool briefly on a wire rack before removing it from the tin. Set aside until completely cool.

8. Slather over the chilled cashew frosting, smoothing it around the sides with a spatula. Finally, decorate with crushed pistachios. The cake is best eaten fresh, but will keep for up to 3 days.

TWO WAYS *with* BANANA BREAD

Selecting which of these banana breads to feature in the book was so impossible that in the end I simply opted to include both. One is 100 percent gluten-free and sweetened mostly with dates, while the other is an out-and-out refined flour/sugar fest that has been a favourite of mine for years. Rest assured, they are equal in stature (and in taste!). Moist, satisfying and ridiculously easy to make, they will quickly become a baking mainstay... or I'll eat my banana-bread-lovin' hat. And while they make for a wonderful dessert, they're equally good breakfast fare, especially with a hot cup of coffee first thing. What can I say, it's the simple pleasures in life – and this is one (or two) of mine.

TIP: Jazz up your bread with some blueberries, chocolate chips or walnuts – simply stir a large handful through the batter before transferring to the loaf tin.

CLASSIC BANANA BREAD
Serves 8–10

300g plain white flour
2 teaspoons baking powder
½ teaspoon bicarbonate of soda
130g light soft brown sugar
3 ripe bananas
120ml Plant Milk (see page 28)
1 teaspoon cider vinegar
50ml agave nectar
80ml sunflower oil

1. Preheat the oven to 170°C/gas mark 3 and grease a 900g loaf tin.
2. Mix the flour, baking powder, bicarbonate of soda and sugar in a large bowl until combined.
3. Mash the bananas to a pulp before whisking in the plant milk, cider vinegar, agave, oil and 1 tablespoon water.
4. Make a well in the centre of the dry ingredients and pour in the banana mixture. Mix together.
5. Transfer to the loaf tin and bake for 45–50 minutes. Leave to cool for at least 10 minutes before removing from the tin. This will keep for up to five days.

GLUTEN-FREE CHOCOLATE BANANA LOAF
GLUTEN FREE
Serves 8–10

130g gram flour
70g ground almonds
2 heaped tablespoons cocoa powder
1 teaspoon gluten-free baking powder
½ teaspoon bicarbonate of soda
pinch of salt
3 Medjool dates, stoned
2 tablespoons maple syrup
2 ripe bananas, mashed
1 tablespoon coconut oil
30g Goji berries (optional)
handful of cacao nibs, to garnish

FOR THE FROSTING:
1 tablespoon coconut oil
2 tablespoons cacao powder
1 tablespoon maple syrup

1. Preheat the oven to 180°C/gas mark 4 and grease a 450g loaf tin.
2. Mix together the dry ingredients in a large bowl.
3. Soak the dates in warm water for 10 minutes.
4. Place the dates in a food processor with the maple syrup. Blitz to form a thick, sticky paste.
5. Whisk the puréed banana, date paste and coconut oil together, along with 2 tablespoons water.
6. Make a well in the centre of the flour and pour in the banana mixture. Fold gently until everything is combined.
7. Stir through the Goji berries before transferring the mixture to a loaf tin. The batter will be quite thick so spread it out using a spatula.
8. Bake for 30–35 minutes. Leave it to cool for 10 minutes before removing from the tin and transferring to a wire rack.
9. For the frosting, melt the coconut oil in a small saucepan and whisk in the cacao powder and maple syrup to form a thick ganache. Spread over the warm loaf. Finish with the cacao nibs.
10. Once cool, cut into thick slices and serve. This is best eaten fresh, but will keep for up to three days.

CARROT *and* WALNUT CAKE

Endlessly moist with a moreish buttercream, this carrot cake holds a special place in my culinary heart – even if it is a bit of a sugar-fest. C'est la vie. I like to think of this as an 'occasion' cake, which means I don't bake it too often. Don't be concerned that it takes rather a long time in the oven... and don't be tempted to take it out early, or you'll find yourself with a raw interior. I like to counteract its unusually long baking time by immediately sealing in the moisture when it comes out. Simply clamp a plate on top of the cake tin to ensure the top and sides don't dry out, leaving you with a super-moist, perfectly crumbly carrot cake. Sugar content be damned.

Serves 8–10

150g finely grated carrot (about 5 carrots)
230g spelt flour
1 teaspoon baking powder
½ teaspoon bicarbonate of soda
pinch of salt
1 teaspoon ground cinnamon
¼ teaspoon freshly grated nutmeg
½ teaspoon ground ginger
120g apple purée
110g light brown sugar
juice of ½ orange
100ml Plant Milk (see page 28)
1 teaspoon vanilla extract
1 tablespoon agave or maple syrup
60ml sunflower or olive oil
50g walnuts, roughly chopped, plus 40g extra to decorate
50g raisins

FOR THE BUTTERCREAM:
100g vegan margarine
300g icing sugar
¼ teaspoon ground ginger
¼ teaspoon ground cinnamon
¼ teaspoon freshly grated nutmeg
grated zest of 1 orange

1. Preheat the oven to 190°C/gas mark 5. Grease a 23cm cake tin.
2. Squeeze out any excess juice from the grated carrots and set aside until needed.
3. Put the flour, baking powder, bicarbonate of soda, salt and spices in a bowl and stir.
4. Place the apple purée, sugar, orange juice, plant milk, vanilla extract, agave or syrup and oil in a large bowl. Whisk thoroughly until the mixture is thick and frothy.

5. Make a well in the centre of the flour, pour in the wet ingredients and fold gently until combined before stirring through the carrots, walnuts and raisins.
6. Transfer the cake batter to the greased tin and tap the tin gently on the work surface to release any air bubbles. Bake for 40 minutes. Leave it to sit on a wire rack for about 10 minutes before removing from the tin. Once the cake has completely cooled, carefully halve it horizontally using a serrated knife.
7. For the buttercream, place the margarine in a large bowl and sift in the icing sugar and spices. Beat vigorously until thick and creamy. Grate in the zest and stir to combine.
8. Spread about a third of the buttercream on the bottom half of the cake, carefully place the other half on top and finish with the remaining buttercream. Use a spatula to spread it evenly over the top of the cake, avoiding going around the edges.
9. Blitz several tablespoons of walnuts to a fine rubble and sprinkle around the edge of the cake. Finish with a whole walnut, if you have one, in the centre. The cake will keep for 3–5 days in an airtight container.

SPICED MOLASSES BUNDT BREAD

Oh mama. This is my kind of bread. Spiced. Sticky. And seriously moreish. I only make it for special occasions for this very reason. Thankfully there's a nutritional plus side to the molasses addition in the form of iron (pregnant ladies take note!) as well as calcium and magnesium, which are both particularly helpful in the prevention of osteoporosis. If you're overly concerned about the sugar content then simply swap it out for your favourite vegan sweetener and whisk it into the wet ingredients. Now go forth and get sticky!

Serves 8–10

TIP: For the purée, place half a butternut squash flesh side down on a baking dish, add a splash of water and cover with foil. Roast in a hot oven (200°C/gas mark 6) for about 1 hour until soft. Spoon out the flesh and blitz to a smooth purée in a blender. This recipe requires 200g purée, so measure it out as your squash may yield a little more.

170g plain white flour
90g buckwheat flour
150g light brown sugar
1 teaspoon bicarbonate of soda
½ teaspoon baking powder
pinch of salt
1 teaspoon ground cinnamon
1 teaspoon allspice
½ teaspoon freshly grated nutmeg
½ teaspoon ground ginger
200g butternut squash purée (see Tip)
60ml olive oil
60ml blackstrap molasses
1 teaspoon vanilla extract

1. Preheat the oven to 170°C/gas mark 3 and grease a 22cm bundt tin.
2. Stir the flours, sugar, bicarbonate of soda, baking powder, salt and spices together in a large bowl.
3. In a separate bowl, thoroughly whisk the puréed squash, oil, molasses, vanilla and 60ml water until smooth.
4. Make a well in the centre of the flour mixture and pour in the wet ingredients. Fold gently until combined, making sure not to overwork the mixture, before transferring to the bundt tin. Tap the tin gently on the work surface to release any air bubbles and bake for 30 minutes.
5. Leave it to rest for about 10 minutes before removing from the tin, then leave to cool completely on a wire rack before serving. The bundt bread will keep for 5–7 days.

STICKY BOURBON BAKLAVA

For me, there are few sweets more tempting than baklava. Usually doused in some sort of buttery honeyed syrup, they are normally out of bounds for us vegans, so it's good to know salvation lies in the homemade sort. I've added the Bourbon because, well, why not? Plus, it gives these nutty, gooey squares of deliciousness a somewhat grown-up feel – liquor will do that to a dish. Granted, this is about as far from health food as you're likely to find but hey, I won't tell if you won't. **Serves 8–10**

15 sheets filo pastry
130g hazelnuts
100g walnuts
1 tablespoon brown sugar
1 teaspoon allspice
fresh grating of nutmeg
215g vegan margarine (or melted coconut oil)

FOR THE SYRUP:
300g unrefined granulated sugar
200g agave nectar or other vegan sweetener of your choosing
60ml pomegranate juice (or orange/cranberry)
1 teaspoon natural orange extract (or orange blossom water)
½ cinnamon stick
3 cloves
1 piece of lemon rind
juice of ½ lemon
100ml Bourbon

1. Preheat the oven to 160°C/gas mark 3.
2. Remove the pastry sheets from the fridge and cover with a clean tea towel so they don't dry out.
3. Blitz the nuts in a food processor with the brown sugar, ½ teaspoon of the allspice and the nutmeg. Set aside, reserving about 1 tablespoon of the mixture to be used for the topping.
4. Melt the vegan margarine and brush onto the bottom of a 30cm rectangular baking dish. Begin to place filo sheets into the tin, brushing with melted margarine as you go. When you have layered 5 sheets into the tin, scatter over an even layer of half of the blended nuts. Repeat the process with another 5 sheets of filo and the remaining nuts, then top with the final 5 sheets, making sure to brush the final sheet with plenty of melted vegan margarine.
5. Cut the pastry now – you can slice it diagonally or into squares, whichever you prefer – then bake for 50–60 minutes until golden. Remove from the oven and leave to cool.
6. When the pastry is completely cool, put all the syrup ingredients, except the Bourbon, in a saucepan and bring to the boil before simmering for 10–15 minutes until the sugar completely dissolves and the syrup reduces. At the very end, add the Bourbon and simmer briefly before taking off the heat and pouring generously over the pastry, making sure it gets between all the cracks.
7. Sprinkle over the remaining crushed nut mixture and allspice powder. Leave it to cool completely before attempting to remove the pieces from the dish using a small spatula – or in my case a butter knife... worked a treat! The baklava will keep for about a week.

MATCHA *and* PECAN COOKIES

The uber green hue of these cookies might be off putting to many but I adore matcha so much I just can't help but include it here. Basically a fancy green tea, matcha is full of antioxidants, but more importantly it also adds a unique layer of flavour to these perfectly chewy morsels. They make a pretty good St Patrick's Day treat, too. **Makes 18 cookies**

90g vegan margarine

110g caster sugar

40g icing sugar

1 teaspoon vanilla extract

juice of ½ lemon

150g plain flour

1 tablespoon matcha powder

¾ teaspoon baking powder

50g chopped pecans

1. Cream the margarine and sugars together in a bowl until fluffy before adding the vanilla extract and lemon juice. Beat thoroughly to combine.

2. Sieve in the flour, matcha and baking powder and mix until it forms a rough dough. Work the pecans into the mixture before turning out onto a clean work surface. Shape the dough into a thick log, wrap in cling film and refrigerate for at least 1 hour.

3. Preheat the oven to 180°C/gas mark 4. Slice or tear off a piece of dough and roll it into a rough ball and place on a baking tray. Repeat until all or most of the dough is used. Flatten each cookie with the back of a fork and bake for 10 minutes.

4. Remove from the oven when they are still soft and carefully transfer to a wire rack. The cookies will keep for 3–5 days in an airtight container.

BEETROOT
and LEMON
CUPCAKES

Delicate flavours are a weakness of mine, especially during the spring and summer months. While you might think beetroot would bring an overbearingly earthy flavour to proceedings, you couldn't be more wrong. Not only do they bring an unprecedented moistness, they also allow the light lemon frosting to really shine. I like to underfill each cupcake case, so as to leave a sufficient gap for frosting, making them feel just that inch more dainty. Tea parties are definitely in our midst. **Makes 6 cupcakes**

110g plain white flour
50g caster sugar, plus 1 tablespoon vanilla sugar (or 60g sugar in total)
¾ teaspoon baking powder
¼ teaspoon bicarbonate of soda
70g pre-cooked vacuum-packed beetroot (not in vinegar)
100ml Plant Milk (see page 28)
1 tablespoon vanilla extract
1 tablespoon melted coconut oil
grated lemon zest, to decorate

FOR THE FROSTING:
150g icing sugar
2 tablespoons vegan margarine
1 tablespoon lemon juice

1. Preheat the oven to 170°C/gas mark 3 and line a muffin tin with 6 muffin cases.
2. Lightly mix the flour, sugar, baking powder and bicarbonate of soda together in a large bowl.
3. Blend the beetroot with the plant milk in a food processor or blender until smooth, then transfer to a separate bowl or jug. Whisk in the vanilla extract and melted coconut oil.
4. Make a well in the centre of the flour mixture and pour in the wet ingredients. Gently fold to incorporate, making sure not to overwork the mixture. Divide evenly between the 6 cupcake cases. Tap gently on the work surface to release any air bubbles.
5. Bake for 20 minutes. Remove from the oven and immediately transfer the cupcakes to a wire rack.
6. While the cupcakes are cooling, make the frosting. Beat the icing sugar, margarine and lemon juice together until smooth. Refrigerate for at least 30 minutes.
7. Once the cupcakes are completely cool and the frosting has been sufficiently chilled, decorate each cupcake using a spatula. Decorate with lemon zest and serve. The cupcakes will keep for 3–5 days.

MACADAMIA *and* BLUEBERRY CREAM PIE

Cashews aren't the only nut that can be given the vegan cream treatment. Macadamias are also rather adept at transforming themselves and, because of their subtle taste, are magnificent for pairing with a variety of ingredients. I tend to err on the sweet side when it comes to these heart-friendly little nuts (like Brazil nuts, they contain the cardio-protective micro-mineral selenium) and my favourite flavour combination is this one because the blueberry compote has the ability to lift the richness of the cream with the deeply fragrant hazelnuts, adding another layer of interest. Feel free to play about, though – simply use the macadamia cream as your base and away you go! Serves 4–6

FOR THE BLUEBERRY COMPOTE:
125g blueberries
juice of ½ lime
2 tablespoons maple syrup

FOR THE HAZELNUT CRUST:
100g hazelnuts, plus extra for the topping
3 stoned Medjool dates

FOR THE MACADAMIA CREAM FILLING:
200g soaked macadamias (see page 120)
1 tablespoon coconut oil
60ml coconut water
60ml agave nectar
juice of 1 lime

1. For the blueberry compote, simmer the blueberries, lime juice and maple syrup in a saucepan until the berries are soft and begin to exude their juices. Before they lose their shape completely, take them off the heat and set aside to cool. Refrigerate until needed.
2. Make the hazelnut crust by pulsing together the hazelnuts and dates until it comes together in a dense sticky rubble. Transfer to a 15cm pie dish or lined brownie tin and evenly spread over the surface area of the dish, pressing down with a spatula or the backs of your fingers. Refrigerate until needed.
3. For the filling, blend the soaked macadamias with the coconut oil, coconut water, agave and lime juice in a food processor or blender until smooth – scraping down the sides periodically and adding a little more coconut water if necessary. It will go through several stages and may require some patience before you achieve the desired consistency.
4. Once it is completely smooth and fluffy, swirl through about 1 tablespoon of the blueberry compote before smoothing out over the chilled crust using the back of a spoon. Refrigerate for at least 1 hour before serving although overnight is best.
5. Crush the extra hazelnuts and sprinkle over the top before serving each slice with an additional spoonful of compote.

MINT CHOC AVOCADO PUD

Sometimes I need something sweet but without any hassle. Desserts like this one are a saviour in such instances and I often double or quadruple the quantities if I'm in the mood for sharing the chocolatey minty love. You don't necessarily need to press it through a sieve but because we are using fresh mint here, it definitely helps in getting that texture silky smooth. Likewise, if you have an aversion to agave, simply double up on the Medjool date quantity for a slightly healthier spin on an already virtually sin-free pud. **Serves 1**

1 small avocado
1 heaped tablespoon raw cacao or cocoa powder
15g fresh mint, plus 1 extra leaf to decorate
1 stoned Medjool date
1 tablespoon agave nectar
1 teaspoon vanilla extract
pinch of sea salt
cacao nibs, to decorate

1. Scoop the avocado flesh into a food processor or mini blender. Add the remaining ingredients and blend until smooth. Check for sweetness and press through a fine-mesh sieve for a smoother finish.
2. Refrigerate for at least 1 hour. Serve in a small bowl and decorate with cacao nibs and a fresh mint leaf.

COCONUT RICE PUDDING

If it's not obvious already then let it be officially known that I love – and I do mean 'LOVE' – coconut. Whether it's fresh, in milk form, desiccated or as a rich cultured yogurt, I'll take it any which way please... and then some more again. This pudding really illuminates the power of this most magnificent of foods and despite only having a smidge of palm sugar to sweeten it, it exudes both decadence and comfort, all in one warming bowl. The maple-flavoured persimmon slices are the perfect accompaniment to what is actually a reasonably virtuous dessert. Which, in foodie code talk, means a second helping for me. Hurrah!

Serves 2–4

130g sushi rice
400ml can coconut milk
1 cinnamon stick
1 star anise
1 vanilla pod
3 cardamom pods
4 tablespoons palm sugar or
   agave nectar
1 persimmon, sharon fruit or mango,
   peeled and sliced
toasted desiccated coconut, to decorate

1. Thoroughly rinse the sushi rice and set aside.
2. Pour the coconut milk into a small saucepan along with 300ml water and bring to a gentle simmer. Add the cinnamon stick, star anise, vanilla pod (scrape the seeds out and add these to the pan too), cardamom pods and sugar. Let the sugar dissolve – this may take a few minutes.
3. Whisk in the rice and stir vigorously in the first few minutes to ensure the kernels don't clump.
4. Cook, uncovered, for 45 minutes or until the rice is cooked through. It is vital you stir frequently to prevent sticking, adding a little water now and then if it appears too thick.
5. Serve the rice pudding hot or cold, topped with sliced persimmon and dessicated coconut.

SIMPLE STRAWBERRY GALETTE

Pastry is one of those things that scares even the most experienced of cooks... after all, that's why most kitchens have a designated pastry chef, because it's essentially an art form in itself, right? This, then, is something of a cheat's recipe that will render the desired dessert result but without having to know the intricacies of how to make the most authentically perfect shortcrust. Sweet, rich, buttery, crumbly – it may not fool Roland Mesnier but it might just convince your guests, and in my little world, that's all that really matters. **Serves 4–6**

200g strawberries, washed and hulled
1 tablespoon icing sugar, plus extra for dusting
½ tablespoon vanilla extract
soya cream, to serve

FOR THE PASTRY:
50g icing sugar
110g plain white flour
50g fridge-cold vegan margarine
1 tablespoon water

1. First, make the pastry. Sieve the icing sugar and flour into a bowl. Add the margarine and work into the flour mixture using your fingertips to lightly incorporate until it resembles very fine breadcrumbs.
2. Add the water and work the mixture into a dough using your hands, adding a little more flour if it is still a bit tacky. Form into a ball, wrap in cling film and refrigerate for about 30 minutes.
3. Put the strawberries in a bowl, sprinkle over the sugar and vanilla and toss. Set aside until the sugar dissolves and juices begin to leach out from the strawberries.
4. Preheat the oven to 180°C/gas mark 4.
5. On a floured surface, roll the dough out into a rough circle about 0.5cm thick and carefully transfer to a floured baking sheet. Spoon the strawberries into the centre of the dough and crease the edges around the fruit – it shouldn't be too neat. Bake for about 40 minutes until cooked and lightly golden, brushing the fruit halfway through with any remaining strawberry juices from the bowl.
6. Transfer to a wire rack and once completely cooled, dust over a little icing sugar. Slice and serve with soya cream.

GLUTEN FREE

BANOFFEE PIE

Everybody loves banoffee pie. An absolute classic, normally known for its intoxicating sweetness and calorific content, this nearly raw (discounting the grated chocolate) equivalent is just as delicious and a heck of a lot healthier. A gluten-free dessert that everyone can enjoy, it's the ultimate vegan treat that will dispel any plant-based myths your dubious guests or family may have. Add it to your recipe armoury pronto and prepare to bask in the inevitable vegan glory. **Serves 2–4**

1 banana, thinly sliced
grated dark chocolate, to top

FOR THE CRUST:
100g pecans
2 stoned Medjool dates
½ tablespoon coconut oil
pinch of salt

FOR THE CARAMEL FILLING:
200g stoned Medjool dates
50ml Plant Milk (see page 28)
2 teaspoons vanilla extract
2 tablespoons water

FOR THE CREAM TOPPING:
220ml coconut cream, refrigerated
1 tablespoon agave nectar

1. Put all the crust ingredients in a food processor or blender and pulse until it comes together in a coarse rubble. Transfer to a 15cm loose-bottomed tart tin and press the crust to the edges, ensuring it is evenly distributed and rises up the sides of the dish. Refrigerate for at least 1 hour or freeze for 15 minutes before carefully removing from the tin and sliding it off the bottom.
2. Put all the filling ingredients in a food processor or blender and blend until completely smooth. For an extra smooth caramel, press through a fine-mesh sieve. Spoon into the crust and refrigerate until needed.
3. Whip the coconut cream and agave until light and fluffy. Refrigerate for around 1 hour until it firms up.
4. Working from the outside in, layer the sliced banana around the caramel, then spoon over the cream – don't spread to the edges, allowing the bananas to peek through. Grate over a little dark chocolate and serve.

TIP: You could use mini tart tins to make individual banoffee pies like the ones shown here.

SIMPLE OATY COOKIES

I like to think these are the very definition of naughty and nice. Soft, chewy rounds of oaty goodness, they're a super little recipe to have up your sleeve when you're pushed for time – and have only a few essential ingredients in the cupboard.

Makes 8 cookies

80g oats
1 teaspoon baking powder
pinch of salt
1 tablespoon coconut oil, melted
4 tablespoons agave nectar or maple syrup
1 teaspoon vanilla extract
1 banana, mashed
handful of raisins

1. Preheat the oven to 180°C/gas mark 4 and line a baking sheet with baking parchment.
2. Mix the oats, baking powder and salt lightly together in a large bowl until combined.
3. Whisk the coconut oil, agave or maple syrup, vanilla extract and mashed banana vigorously together until combined.
4. Pour the wet ingredients into the flour mixture and gently fold together. Stir through the raisins.
5. Drop a tablespoonful onto the prepared baking sheet and flatten slightly with the back of a fork. Repeat until all the batter is used – it should render about 7–8 cookies.
6. Bake for 20–25 minutes. Remove from the oven and leave to cool completely on a wire rack. The cookies will keep for several days in an airtight container.

SMUGGLERS' HOT COCOA *with* SWEETENED WHIPPED COCONUT CREAM

GLUTEN FREE

This recipe is dedicated to 'The Last of the Cornish Smugglers' (you know who you are!) who braved the deep for their little bit of treasure, hehe. In all seriousness though, I have a weird obsession with smugglers and pirates... which probably has something to do with where I live. Here, in the depths of Cornwall I'm surrounded by stories and tales of times gone by that fuel my imagination – and my food, hence my fondness for rum and cider. This rum-spiked cocoa is a favourite of ours that is best enjoyed curled up on the sofa watching re-runs of *Poldark* – or *Jamaica Inn*, take your pick. Can I get an 'arrr'?! Serves 2

500ml soya milk (or other Plant Milk, see page 28)
1 tablespoon cocoa powder
2 tablespoons agave nectar
1 tablespoon maple syrup
1 cinnamon stick
60ml dark rum

FOR THE CREAM:
125ml coconut cream
1 teaspoon vanilla extract
½ tablespoon agave nectar

TO FINISH:
1 teaspoon ground cinnamon
¼ teaspoon freshly grated nutmeg
¼ teaspoon ground ginger

1. First make the cream. Put the coconut cream in the refrigerator overnight. The next day, add the vanilla extract and agave and lightly whip together. Refrigerate until needed.
2. Put the soya milk in a saucepan and whisk in the cocoa powder until frothy and combined. Add the agave, maple syrup and cinnamon stick and heat gently until it just begins to simmer.
3. Simmer for 5–10 minutes until the milk is sufficiently hot. Remove from the heat and whisk in the rum. Return to a low heat for a minute or two.
4. Divide between 2 cups or bowls and carefully spoon in the coconut cream... it will initially sink but then rise to the top. Mix the spices together and lightly dust over the cocoa.

VEGAN BEAUTY

TOMATO and TAHINI FACE PACK
MINT *and* ROSE WATER FACIAL MIST
BANANA *and SUGAR BODY SCRUB*
WHIPPED COCONUT OIL BODY MOISTURISER
SOOTHING OATMEAL and AVOCADO EXFOLIATOR
BASIL *and* SEA SALT FOOT SCRUB
ORANGE BLOSSOM BATH MILK
THE VEGAN WARDROBE

CRUELTY-FREE BEAUTY

Looking after my skin has always been something of an ongoing obsession but I never really stopped to think about what I was using or the process it has gone through. Turning vegan, of course, changed all that. For the first time ever I was searching for bunny logos and researching brands to ensure they were 'cruelty free'. Thankfully, it is becoming much easier to glean such information making beauty shopping stress free.

I always maintain that given the choice, people would much rather purchase a product that has not been tested on animals – this is something that transcends veganism in my opinion. Brands are not in the habit, however, of advertising the methods they use to test such products and so consumers are deliberately kept in the dark. We are essentially buying blindly. Because of this, I keep a list on my iPhone of brands to avoid that I can refer to with ease… there are also dozens of websites including PETA's 'Cruelty-free List', which is an absolute godsend for keeping you on the straight and narrow.

The crazy thing about the beauty industry is that for all its 'advances' and (hollow, ahem) promises, it's actually decades behind the times when it comes to testing. Established brands seem to be eternally hurrying to catch up on smaller, independent companies that, for the most part, eschew any type of animal testing whatsoever – because, let's face it, it's totally unnecessary. We are now at the stage where we have the means to test products without resorting to animal cruelty and yet, bizarrely, we

still do it. The late Anita Roddick (a personal heroine of mine) realised this way back in the 1980s when she first opened The Body Shop, taking a global outspoken stance against animal testing within the industry. Little did she know how far ahead of her time she really was – here we are in the 21st century, still dithering behind. The mind truly boggles. And yes, The Body Shop has since changed hands (its parent company is currently not 'cruelty-free') meaning it is now out of bounds for many vegans. Sob.

Fear not though. As a vegan, you can still indulge your inner beauty junkie, be it in the form of shop-bought products (preferably organic and paraben-free) or DIY concoctions that require little effort but are still massively effective. I usually make half my products (body scrubs, facial sprays etc.) and buy the rest (shampoo, soap etc.). You'll notice my beauty recipes require only a handful of ingredients, because I rely on what's to hand in my kitchen and rarely, if ever, buy specific oils and 'add-ins'.

Nature has already handed us everything we need to keep our skin looking clear, smooth and supple, so it quietly horrifies me to think of the amount of chemicals I used to layer on my face and body. Of course, makeup can be a bit of a stumbling block when it comes to DIY (I did come across a recipe for foundation once that involved cocoa powder but even my inner hippy was crying 'no!'). At the moment, it's a step too far even for me, and so I stick to the few vegan makeup brands on the market… don't worry, even major pharmacies stock them (and some high-end brands are suitable – hurrah!) – just be sure to check the label or research beforehand. I have a few favourites but am always willing to try new products, as long as they meet my ethical standards. Thankfully, my makeup routine is pretty basic so all I really require is a good concealer, foundation, powder, liquid liner and mascara – this hasn't changed in forever and I doubt I will switch it up anytime soon.

I hope these 'recipes' come in handy and offer up a more natural (wallet-friendly) alternative to fill in some of those cruelty-free beauty gaps that can be tricky in those early stages of veganism. They've become an essential part of my natural beauty routine and I'm always expanding my catalogue… try using them as a jumping-off point yourself and experiment with ingredients you have to hand. Who knows what delights await!

TOMATO *and* TAHINI FACE PACK

When my skin started to look and feel a little drier and more difficult to control, I decided to turn to more natural ways of caring for my skin, with this Tomato and Tahini Face Pack quickly becoming one of my many 'well blow me down with a feather, it actually works' triumphs. I usually opt to use a facepack like this once a week – any more is overkill in my opinion – and tend to leave it on for the duration of my bath, although 10 minutes at a push will suffice. If you suffer from uneven skin tone like me (ah, the joys of being in your thirties) then this is an absolute godsend, as it deals with any noticeable blemishes while also brightening the skin. If I've got a big event coming up, I'll use this pack a couple of days before for radiant skin that makes applying make-up on the day a cinch.

Enough for 3 face packs

1 tomato
1 tablespoon tahini

1. Place the tomato in a cup and cover with freshly boiled water. Set aside for several minutes until the skin becomes blistered. Carefully peel the skin away from the flesh. Halve the tomato and remove the seeds.
2. Transfer the tomato to a pestle and mortar and muddle until it becomes pulp-like. Add the tahini and thoroughly combine.
3. Apply about one-third of the mixture to your face and wash off with lukewarm water after about 10 minutes. Your skin should look brighter and your skin-tone more even. This doesn't keep well, so use immediately.

MINT *and* ROSE WATER FACIAL MIST

Facial mists are a crucial part of my beauty kit. Not only are they terrific for freshening up throughout the day, they're also great for leaving your skin looking perfectly dewy after you've applied your makeup in the morning. This mint and rose water infusion is so simple it barely even counts as a recipe... plus, it's much more cost-effective than forking out for expensive over-the-counter spritzers and does exactly the same job. Once you've invested in your small spray bottle (psst, they're super cheap on the internet) you're officially good to go! **Makes 350ml**

120ml filtered water
several fresh mint sprigs
3 tablespoons rose water

1. Bring the filtered water to the boil in a saucepan. Put the mint leaves in a tall heatproof jar or glass and cover with the freshly boiled water. Leave it to infuse until the water has sufficiently cooled.
2. Once cooled, remove the mint leaves and add the rose water. Place a lid on the jar and shake vigorously, then decant into a small spritzer bottle.
3. Use throughout the day as a refreshing facial spritz or lightly mist over freshly applied makeup to set. This mist will keep for a month in a sealed bottle.

BANANA *and* SUGAR BODY SCRUB

Exfoliation is a huge part of my skincare regime, with this simple body scrub taking centre stage in keeping my arms and legs super smooth. I prefer to use caster sugar as I find it's not overly abrasive on the skin. While I'm sure you're recoiling in horror at the sheer amount of sugar required, just remember that it's not going 'in' your body, just 'on' it. The banana purée is also very hydrating, which will leave your body feeling wonderfully moisturised and instantly revive dull, tired skin. Time to get mashing! **Enough for 5 full body scrubs**

1 small banana
300–375g golden caster sugar

1. Mash the banana to a smooth purée on a chopping board and gradually work in the sugar. As fruit can vary, it may take only 300g of the sugar to achieve the desired scrub consistency but slightly riper/runnier bananas may require the full amount.
2. Once you have a thick, scoop-able scrub consistency, work it into damp skin in a clockwise motion, making sure to focus on problem areas such as the back of the arms. Rinse off thoroughly and enjoy the new smooth you. This scrub will keep in the fridge for 5–7 days.

WHIPPED COCONUT BODY BUTTER

Coconut oil is an absolute godsend for dry skin, leaving it nourished, soft and hydrated for hours. It's anti-ageing, antioxidant benefits are simply the icing on the cake, as it were, but it's this 'whipped' variety I'm particularly nutty about because of its indulgent appeal. For not much effort, you can forgo any chemical-laden body moisturiser and opt for this natural homemade variety instead. I've boosted its 'beauty junkie' appeal by adding a dash of good-quality vanilla extract. Best of all, a little goes a very long way. I predict it won't be long before you're a coconut convert too.
Enough for 20 full body rubs

5 tablespoons unmelted coconut oil
1 teaspoon vanilla extract

1. Place the coconut oil in a medium bowl and whisk vigorously for several minutes until it forms soft peaks – you can use either a hand or an electric whisk.
2. Add the vanilla extract and whisk further to fully amalgamate. When it is sufficiently soft and 'whipped', transfer to a clean jar and store in a cool place to prevent it from melting. However, if it is stored at too cool a temperature it will harden.
3. Massage a small amount into your skin after bathing. This moisturiser will keep for several months in a sealed jar.

SOOTHING OATMEAL *and* AVOCADO EXFOLIATOR

Having sensitive skin means I would never dare use a sugar scrub on my face. Oats are a great alternative in such instances, as they are much more gentle but still manage to smooth out any roughness. The avocado will not only leave your skin feeling totally nourished but it also lends a few other bona fide beauty benefits in the process... it's regarded as being an excellent natural solution to dehydrated skin, as well as helping to protect your skin against sun damage. I tend to use this exfoliator mostly on my face but it also works really well on upper arms too – because it can be quite thick, be sure to warm it between your hands before applying to damp skin and await the soothing post-scrub glow. **Enough for 1–2 facepacks**

½ avocado, peeled and stoned
30g porridge oats (or reserved plant milk 'oat-meal', see page 26)

1. Mash the avocado flesh in a bowl with the back of a fork until smooth and creamy.
2. Pulse the oats in a food processor or mini blender to break them up, making sure they still retain some nubbly texture.
3. Add the oats to the mashed avocado and stir.
4. Splash your face with a little water to dampen before applying. Take a generous amount of the avocado mixture and warm it between your hands to loosen. Work it into the skin in a gentle circular motion.
5. Rinse with lukewarm water and allow your skin to air dry before applying a facial oil or moisturiser. This doesn't keep well, so use immediately.

BASIL *and* SEA SALT FOOT SCRUB

This basil and sea salt combination is by far my favourite treat for feet, and works wonderfully on those hard spots that are difficult to get rid of. Basil might seem like a strange ingredient in a foot scrub but, seeing as it belongs to the mint family, it actually makes perfect sense. But it's not just its aromatic qualities I'm after, because basil actually has an array of benefits when applied to the skin... in particular, it possesses some healing and antiseptic properties that make it the perfect pairing for tired and forgotten tootsies. Likewise, the sea salt is abrasive enough to shift any unwanted dead skin without causing lesions or damage, with the olive oil lending that ultimate Mediterranean moisturising factor, leaving your feet feeling silky smooth and refreshed. **Enough for 5 foot scrubs**

50g fresh basil
juice of 1 lemon
100g sea salt
30ml olive oil

1. Muddle the basil and lemon juice together in a pestle and mortar. Strain the liquid through a small sieve or tea strainer into a bowl.
2. Add the sea salt and olive oil and whisk until combined before applying liberally to both feet.
3. Work the mixture into the soles of your feet, focusing particularly on the heels and ball of each foot. Massage both feet twice, allowing the salt and oil to really absorb into the skin.
4. Rinse with lukewarm water and lightly towel dry or, if possible, let your feet dry naturally. This scrub will keep for 2 weeks in a sealed jar.

ORANGE BLOSSOM BATH MILK

It's amazing how such simple pairings can produce something so decadent. Inspired by Cleopatra with her famously indulgent 'milk and honey' baths, this vegan version is equally luxurious and has more than a few beauty benefits too. Not only is the orange blossom water perfect for sensitive skin, its mildly astringent properties means it will both soothe and rejuvenate. As for the almond milk, its Vitamin E credentials make it the ultimate bath addition, keeping any skin problems such as acne or prickly skin at bay, as well as being one of nature's great moisturisers. Move over 'milk and honey', it's time to give bathing a plant-based makeover. **Enough for 1 bath**

100g whole almonds
2 tablespoons orange blossom water

1. Blend the almonds with twice the amount of water to nuts, then strain through a nut milk bag or muslin cloth.
2. Whisk in the orange blossom water and set it aside to amalgamate for about 30 minutes.
3. Pour the milk into the bath while the water is running, making sure to disperse it before enjoying an indulgent, calming soak. If you don't want to use the bath milk straight away, it will keep for a few days in the fridge.

THE VEGAN WARDROBE

Let's talk clothes. As a self-confessed consumer of all things pretty, this is an aspect of veganism that was a slow burner for me. No, I didn't immediately clear out my wardrobe of all things 'animal based' – instead I whittled away until, some four or so years later, I have a virtually cruelty-free closet (barring a few silk scarves that have sentimental value and a couple of tatty old wool jumpers that are yet to be donated) – that's my lot.

In keeping with my overall approach to veganism, I understand that everyone's stance will be slightly different. Some of you will feel the urge to do a complete closet cleanse, getting rid of any and all of your past life and that's cool. Hats off to ya. Personally, I didn't have the budget to replace many of the items I had so dearly collected over the years, including leather boots, bags and the like, so I waited until they had served their purpose while collating the funds to do a more ethically sound fashion swap.

Having acquired a healthy stash of clothes over many, many years, it was at times hard (read unbearable) to part with some of the more unique items. However, being in Chicago at the time of my 'transition' meant I could easily trade those clothes for equally awesome ones at places like Buffalo (a vintage store that buys, sells and trades clothing). I also sold more 'expensive' items on sites like eBay, although nowadays there are a variety of better websites that deal in such things. In the end, once I had rid myself of these material ties to my previous life as an all-singing, all-dancing shopaholic, I felt freer than I had done in years. There was no going back and a new era was emerging before me – one that still allowed me to indulge in a little retail therapy and express myself through style, but with a slightly more considered mindset.

Several years down the line and, while I still haven't perfected my purchasing habits, I've certainly made many discoveries along the way. High-street shops are not necessarily out of bounds but I do try to ensure that I will get at least 30 wears out of each item – you wouldn't believe how much this reduces waste and has saved me from buying 'trendy' items I'll get bored with in about a month. I also religiously check labels to ensure they haven't sneaked any wool or angora (i.e. rabbit hair) into the mix and rarely impulse buy, preferring to mull things over before handing over any cash. All of which has helped me pare down my wardrobe to one that is much more manageable and refined... I still add my little retro flourishes but there is definitely a simplicity to my personal style that wasn't there before.

When I can, I try to buy from independent designers that have an eco-friendly ethos but more often it's off to the charity shop I go in a bid to recycle other people's unwanted tat. I've always relished scouring those mish-mashed rails of chaos on a quest to find that authentic mid-century dress for a song. I realise that second-hand shopping isn't for everyone, but that doesn't mean your only option is to buy fast fashion that will inevitably be headed for the landfill. Not only do these pieces have a human cost, they also harm the environment. Set your sights a little higher and aim to buy quality items now and again instead. As Dame Vivienne Westwood would say, 'Don't invest in fashion, invest in the world'.

While we're on the topic of the environment, let's take a moment to discuss the great divider... 'man-made' fabrics. Yes, it's true, as vegans we shun wool and leather, sometimes replacing them with synthetic materials that are known to be environmentally harmful. Not good. So, are there any other options available to us? Well, I'm delighted to say, yes! Just because we can't (or won't) partake in animal-based fibres doesn't mean our only option is to contribute to the demise of our planet. I aim to buy mostly 'natural fibres' such as cotton, linen, hemp or bamboo although there are many more being developed, including tencel (sometimes called lyocell), which is a sustainable fabric made from wood pulp. Likewise, the 'vegan leather' market is breaking new ground with new materials that are both breathable and biodegradable. Look out for shoes and bags that are made from cork, barkcloth, glazed cotton and even degradable polyurethane, which is part-recycled, solvent free and uses much less energy than traditional PU. Of course, this is not a perfect solution to a complex scenario but shows that we are inching closer to a better alternative.

To give this debate a little more context, the leather industry also has huge environmental drawbacks directly linked to the hazardous chemicals used in the 'tanning' process, which is actually what preserves the skin in order for it not to degrade too soon. And if you think the wool industry is any better, let me briefly draw your attention to 'mulesing', a practice used in Australia (where the majority of our wool comes from) to prevent flystrike. Studies have shown that this practice causes a great deal of distress to the animal, and while it is not common practice worldwide, I would rather wear the odd bit of acrylic than risk a merino sweater purchase that could easily come with a pain-filled price-tag. This is where I draw my line but yours might very well be different, so my only real advice is to first arm yourself with the facts and then come to your own informed conclusion.

Fur, too, is most likely at the forefront of your new-found veganism (or curiosity) and rightly so. Whereas leather is arguably a byproduct of the meat industry, fur is solely about breeding animals for the purpose of fashion. It's a cruel, unnecessary practice that I personally want no part of... and with faux fur companies springing up left, right and centre, I think (hope) it will soon be phased out. It's a simple case of supply and demand. As consumers we are at the root of this chain, which, if you think about it, is a pretty powerful place to be.

Whether your ideals flow over into all areas of your life is really up to you – like I said before, everybody has their line, so it's merely up to you to decide where to ultimately draw it. You may feel anxious about how others will perceive you if you 'eat this' or 'wear that' and it takes a lot of strength to quiet that noise – and truly, that is all it is.

At times like these, step away from social media and allow yourself some space from all this new information. As an industry, cruelty-free fashion is in its infancy and evolving all the time, so even experienced vegans won't have all the answers at their fingertips. Having spent a number of years working within the fashion industry myself, I feel like I've got to see how things work first hand. Great design inspires me, and remains a huge passion, but I try not to put my consumerist desires ahead of my ethical credentials, and while that sounds terribly boring that doesn't mean I still don't have fun with my style. Balance is key when it comes to clothing, and your vegan wardrobe needn't be all tie-dye and sandals. I always try to experiment with what I already own and sporadically add special pieces that will transform more than one outfit.

It's important to remember that fashion is an extension of our personality – it's how we express ourselves and sends out a direct message about who we are and what we stand for. The only difference now being, that message is equal parts substance and style.

INDEX

ACKNOWLEDGEMENTS

First and foremost, thanks to everyone at Kyle Books for their wonderful work on this book... in particular, a huge thank you goes to my Editor, Tara O'Sullivan, who has been endlessly open to my ideas and an integral part in bringing them all to fruition. Thanks also to Kyle for her continuing support.

A massive thanks goes to Nassima Rothacker for her mindblowing photography prowess and boundless creativity on this project... it was a pleasure and a privilege working with you. A flurry of further 'thank yous' to the remainder of the 'dream team', including Aya Nishimura and Tony Hutchinson for their styling genius, and not forgetting the bevy of incredible assistants who made everything go without a hitch, including Katrina Alexander, Sam Dixon, Emma Godwin and Sian Henley.

Thanks to Helen Bratby for making the book look so darn beautiful... I'm in awe of your superb design skills and ever grateful for all your work on the book. A big shout-out to Stuart Simpson, too, for his sensational illustrations – they are dreamy perfection!

I would also like to thank Abi Waters for making sure every 'i' was dotted and 't' was crossed... your eye for detail has left no stone unturned.

Closer to home, I'd like to thank my spectacular family (Mum, Dad and Mairead) for always staying positive, even when my confidence waivered... I feel truly blessed to have three such special people in my life. Big Love.

Finally, a colossal, heartfelt thank you to my beautiful husband Jason for putting up with my cookbook induced craziness– your strength makes everything easier. None of this would be possible without you. I love you.